Baltimore County, Maryland
TRADER
and
ORDINARY LICENSES
1830 - 1832

Michael A. Ports

Copyright © 2013
Michael A. Ports
All Rights Reserved

Published for Clearfield Company by
Genealogical Publishing Company
Baltimore, Maryland 2013

ISBN 978-0-8063-5654-9

Made in the United States of America

Table of Contents

Introduction	1
Traders Licenses	5
Ordinary Licenses	12
Baltimore County Boundaries	24
License Fees and Terms	25
Turnpikes and Taverns	28
Tabulation	31
Annapolis Road	33
Washington Turnpike	34
Baltimore and Ohio Railroad	36
Frederick Turnpike	38
Liberty Road	46
Reisterstown (or Hookstown) Turnpike	52
Hanover Turnpike	60
Westminster Turnpike	67
Deer Park Road	70
Falls Road Turnpike	71
York Turnpike	75
Harford Turnpike	86
Bel Air Turnpike	91
Philadelphia Turnpike	94
Back River Neck Road	97
Middle River Neck Road	98
Other Locations	99
Index	107

Introduction

The following material is taken directly from the original Baltimore County Court Records.[1] The subject volume of license records contains a total of nineteen pages. The front cover of the volume is labeled *"Traders Licenses"* and the back cover is labeled *"Ordinary Licenses."* The trader license entries begin on the first page and proceed in chronological order, while the ordinary license entries begin on the last page and proceed in chronological order backwards toward the middle of the volume. While the pages of the original volume are not numbered, the following transcription is numbered sequentially as if the pages were numbered. The pages of trader licenses are presented in both numerical sequence from [1] through [7] and in chronological order from May 1, 1830 through April 5, 1832. The pages of ordinary licenses are presented in chronological order, but in reverse numerical order from [19] through [8].

Every effort has been made to transcribe the names and residences as faithfully and accurately as possible. No attempt has been made to correct any spelling or capitalization errors. In general, the handwriting in the original is legible and not too difficult to decipher. In most cases, the clerk entered each name in its natural order, only occasionally reversing the order by entering the surname first. Thus, the entry that reads Cooper Tego probably should have been entered as Tego Cooper in order to be consistent with the majority of the other entries, likewise for Linnard Zeney, John Leef, and Ann Moran.

Each license entry includes the date, name of licensee, residence of the licensee, and amount paid. By far, most of the residence locations are described by a mile post, or distance along, a particular turnpike, road, or other location descriptor, a few having additional notations. Some of the mile post locations are recorded as near the subject road, implying the licensee resided or conducted business at some

---

[1] Baltimore County Court, License Records, Traders & Ordinary Licenses, 1830-1832, MSA No. C366-2, MdHR No. 40,101-2. Maryland State Archives, Annapolis, Maryland.

unspecified distance from the subject road. Other locations are simply described by the name of a place, such as Canton or Oakland Mills.

The license entries apparently were entered in chronological order. Rather than signifying the date the clerk made the entry, the date more likely signifies the effective date of the license fee. Thus, a particular entry probably was made sometime after the date entered. The clerk made liberal use of ditto marks when recording the licenses. The ditto marks in the date columns are transcribed as originally recorded; however, the ditto marks in the residence column are not, instead replaced with the words intended. The prudent researcher is cautioned to check the original document for alternate interpretations.

During the subject era, a trader was not a shopkeeper or other retailer; rather, a trader was akin to a wholesaler or other middleman. Only forty-nine licenses were issued to traders in 1830. The following year, a total of one hundred fifty-three licenses were issued; but, only eight were issued in 1832, undoubtedly, the records for 1830 and 1832 incomplete. Of the forty-nine licenses issued in 1830, forty-five were issued to individuals, the remaining four issued to business concerns. Two of the forty-five licenses were issued to women. Of the one hundred fifty-three licenses issued in 1831, eight were issued to business concerns and another eight licenses were issued to women. In 1832, out of only eight recorded licenses, one was issued to a business concern and none were issued to women.

It is curious that the licensed establishments were called ordinaries, an obsolete term for tavern even during that era. In other contemporary records, such establishments were called taverns, inns, hotels, or houses, but never ordinaries. The ordinary license entries are presumed to begin in 1830, just as the trader license entries begin. That year, one hundred five licenses were issued for ordinaries, in 1831 two hundred twenty-six licenses were issued, and in 1832 only fifteen licenses were issued, again the records apparently incomplete. Because so many of the licensees, both traders and ordinaries, were licensed at the same location in subsequent years, the licenses appear to have been required on an annual basis.

None of the licensees appear to be residents of Baltimore City, as no locations on city streets are cited in the record, the city as an incorporated municipality apparently issued licenses separately. Along each turnpike, numbered stones were erected at one-mile intervals providing the distance to the courthouse, then in Baltimore City. The mile post distances not associated with a turnpike appear to be the direct line distances in miles from the courthouse, to the residences in question, rather than the actual distances along a road or other location identifier. The direct line distances from the courthouse may be found on the published 1877 Atlas of Baltimore County.[2]

The reader will note that numerous names appear on both the trader and ordinary lists and will recognize the names of the roads and turnpikes recorded by the clerk, as most of the same names, in one form or another, remain in use today. However, the reader is cautioned that the name, precise location, and limits of the early roads and turnpikes have changed substantially over the past 180 years. Early maps, deeds, and other records should be consulted to determine the former location and limits of the various roads and turnpikes with any precision. The reader also should be cautioned that the mile posts cited in the original record are approximate. For example, the eight licensees listed at Mile Post 16 on the Reisterstown Turnpike were not situated check-by-jowl next to one another precisely at that distance along the turnpike. Instead, the eight were situated in or very near to the town of Reisterstown, usually described as sixteen miles from Baltimore. Moreover, numerous ordinaries were named for a mile post, such as Fourteen Mile House; but, the reader should be alerted that such establishments were not necessarily situated immediately adjacent to their namesake milestone, some simply closer to their namesake stone than to another.

---

[2] *Atlas of Baltimore County, Maryland, Surveyed & Published under the Direction of C. M. Hopkins, C. E., 320 Walnut Street, Philadelphia, 1877.* Reproduced from the originals at the Maryland State Archives by the Office of Central Services, Baltimore County, Maryland, 1968.

Following the transcription of the original lists, a series of tables are presented combining the two lists and arranging the licensees in order by mile post along each of the major turnpikes and roads. The tables allow the researcher to locate the licensee in terms of nearby modern landmarks as well as to place many of the licensees among their neighbors. The landmarks, consisting mostly of modern street intersections, necessarily are approximate, due to changes in road alignment and the proximity of modern landmarks; and should not be interpreted with any precision. While most of the major turnpikes and roads of 1830 generally follow the same routes today, the reader is cautioned that there are far too many exceptions to identify and describe all of the significant differences. Following each table, a brief description of the turnpike, road, or location is presented, including the general alignment and mile posts, brief history, any errors or other anomalies found in the original records, and a few simple statistics describing the licensees. Also included are descriptions of some of the old taverns, inns, and hotels, as well as some of the identified mills, factories, and other businesses.

Thank you, Marcia, for your encouragement and support during the long publications process. After all is said and done, it was your idea.

[1]   1830   Traders Licenses

date	To whom granted	Residence	$12 Price p^d
May 1	Wm Jameson	23 miles Westminster road	$12
" "	John Devries	Valley Mills, 20 miles from Balt^o	
" "	Kinsey Johns	18 miles Falls Turnpike	
" "	George Motter	30 miles Reisters turnpike	
" "	William Garey	18 miles Liberty road	
" "	Jon^a Ellicott & Sons	Ellicott's Mills	
" "	Wright & Bailey	13 miles, near old Fred^k road	
" "	John Burnham	13 miles Falls Turnpike	
" "	John Leaf	15 miles Falls Turnpike	
" "	Joshua Gorsuch	19 miles York Turnpike	
" "	Saml Webb	16 miles Manor Turnpike	
" "	Mahlon C. Price	17 miles York Turnpike	
" "	Richard Paine	8 miles Back River Turnpike	
" "	Elisha Battee	2 miles Bel Air Turnpike	
" "	Francis Blackwell	8 miles Reisters' Turnpike	
" "	Thomas Wallace	7 miles York Turnpike	
" "	Jesse Manning	13 miles Hooks Town Turnpike	
" "	Lemuel Garner	22 miles Westminster Turnpike	
" "	Benjn Burk & Son	15 miles old Philadelphia Turnpike	
" "	James Perrigo	8 miles York Turnpike	
" "	Nimrod Chapman	16 miles Reisters' Turnpike	
	One name omitted		
" "	Charity Thompson	8 miles Frederick road	
" "	Upton Reid	16 at Franklinville	
" "	John Zimmerman	30 miles old York road	
" "	Wm Owings	7 miles Frederick road	
" "	Wm Tipton	21 miles York road	
" "	Wm Roe	21 miles York road	
" "	Amos harp	8 miles old Forge road	
" "	Aquila Sparks	30 miles old Harford road	
" "	Laban Welch	5 miles Reisters road	
" "	Otho Shipley	20 miles Liberty road	
" "	Martico M. Welch	25 miles Deer Park road	
	~~Eliz Young~~		
" "	Elijah Burton	7 miles old Harford road	
" "	Sarah Allen	10 miles Liberty road	

[2]

May 1		John Ware	20 miles Liberty road
"		Wm Odell	15 miles near Liberty road
"		Robert Ward	15 miles Liberty road
"		~~Geo: Gelbach~~	~~2½ old Harford road~~
"		Jeremiah Ducker	16 Reisters' road
"		Peter G. Hunter	23 miles at mine run mills
"		Jo^s Stansbury	26 miles near Westminster road
"		George Beckley	24 miles old York road
"		Saml Morton & Son	18 miles Oakland Factory
"		David Hoover	24 miles Falls road
"		Alexis Green	16 miles old York Road
"		Michael McBlair	16 miles Bel Air road
"		Edward Gray	9½ miles Frederick road
"		Aquila Jarvis	3 miles Frederick road
"		Nathan Chapman	17½ near Reisters Town
" 22		Solomon Choate	16 miles Reisterstown $11.30

Traders Licenses 1831

1	May 2	Wright & Bailey	13 miles near old Fred: road $
2	"	Samuel Harlan	2 miles Frederick road
3	"	Ishmael Day	14 miles near Bel Air road
4	"	Martico Merryman Welch	25 miles Deer Park
5	"	Laban Welch	5 miles Balt^o & Reisters
6	"	Paul Rust	4½ miles Franklin
7	"	Francis Blackwell	8 miles Reisters'
8	"	Mordicai G. Cockey	20 miles Westminster
9	"	Eliz^a Stapleton	2 miles Phil^a
10	"	Wesley Driver	8 miles old Frederick
11	"	Samuel Owens	6½ Frederick
12	"	Larkin Young	14 Liberty Road
13	"	Solomon Choate	16 Reisters Town road
14	"	John B. Devries	20 Valley Mills
15	"	William Garey	15 Deer Park road

[End of Original Page]

[3] 1831 Traders Licenses Continued

16	May 2	Frederick Kauffman	27 miles York Road
17	"	Reid Upton	16 miles Franklin Mill
18	"	Cooper Tego	28 miles old York road
19	"	Richd Owings	9 miles Court road
20	"	Elisha Battee	2 miles Bel Air road
21	"	Wm Roe	21 miles York road
22	"	George Bond	27 miles York road
23	"	James Wilson	22 miles York road
24	"	Richard Pearce	6½ miles at Powhattan Factory
25	"	Charles Ford	5 miles old Frederick road
26	"	Mary Brochans	2½ miles Phil^a road
27	"	John Michael	30 miles old York
28	"	Nimrod Chapman	16 miles Reisters Town
29	"	John Burnham	13 miles Falls road
30	"	Benjamin Lesourd	24 miles near Hunter's Mill
31	"	George Motter	30 Hanover Road
32	"	Samuel Webb	16 miles old York road
33	"	Beale Buckingham	31 Liberty road
34	"	Joshua Gorsuch	19 miles York
35	"	John Zimmerman	30 miles near old York road
36	"	Samuel Watkins	16 miles Harford
37	"	Otho Shiply	20 miles Liberty
38	"	Ely Scott	16 miles Falls
39	"	Mahlon C. Price	17 miles York
40	"	Wm Jameson	23 miles Westminster road
41	"	Richard Paine	8 miles Back river
42	"	Baker & Houck	30 miles Hanover Road
43	"	Thomas King	16 miles Old York
		~~James Perrigo~~	~~7 York Road~~
43	"	James Perrigo	8 York road
44	"	Thomas Christopher	12 miles Philadelphia road
45	"	Lemuel Garner	13 miles Reisterstown road
46	"	Thomas Parlett	11 miles Harford road
47	"	George Everhart	30½ miles Hanover road
48	"	Thomas Uppercou	21 miles Hanover road

[4] Traders Licenses Continued

49	May 2	William Wooden	19 Hanover Road
50	"	Jesse Manning	22 Westminster Road
51	"	James Thomas	16 Reisters Town
	"	Edmund Garner	24 Westminster Road
53	"	Joseph Stansbury	25 Westminster Road
	"	Micajah Tracey	3 York Road
	"	Margaret McElhert	16 Reisters' town Road
	"	John Morrow	14 Reisterstown Road
	"	Jonathan Ellicott & Sons	10 Ellicott Mills
	"	Philip Waggoner	9 Reisters Town road
	"	Andrew Burk	23 Hanover
	"	Kinsey Johns	18 Falls Road
	"	Dixon Morton	21 Old York
	"	Saib Devries	13 miles near Balt^{o} & Ohio railroad
	"	David Peden & Co	6 miles Falls
	"	Nicholas Cornelius	10½ York
	"	Catherine Chambers	20 Liberty Road
	"	Jonathan Vanhorn	13½ Phil^{a} Road
	"	John M. Wheat	2 miles Washington
	"	Joshua Spindler	24 miles York
	"	Amelia B. Gill	18 miles Falls road
	"	Jeremiah Ducker	16 miles Reisters' town
	"	Nathan H. Ware	7 miles York road
	"	John Coleman	27 Westminster Road
	"	William Tipton	21 York Road
	"	Samuel J. Gainson	14 Manor Road
	"	James S. Wilson	Long Green near Copper Factory
	"	Thomas Ward	20 Westminster Road
	"	Peter Ewing	24 old York Road
	"	George Bramwell	28 Hanover Road
	"	John Murry J	28 Hanover Road
	"	Jacob Ebaugh	28 Hanover Road

[End of Original Page]

[5] Traders Licenses Continued

82	May 2	John Ware	2 Liberty Road
83	"	Edward Gray	9½ Fred^k Road
84	"	Thomas Porter	16 Deer Park Road
85	"	Joshua Standiford	27 York Road
86	"	Nicholas Harrison	28 miles Hanover Road
87	"	Elijah Burton	7 miles Old Harford Road
88	"	William Barnett	7 miles Old Liberty
89	"	Peter G. Hunter	24 near Wise burg
90	"	Price Nehemiah	14 York Road
91	"	Michael McBlair	16 Bel Air Road
92	"	Sarah Allen	14 Liberty Road
93	"	Amos Earp	8 miles, old Forge road
~~94~~	"	~~Chainey Brooks~~	
94	"	E. G. Kilbourne	14 York Road
95	"	Samuel Penny	12 old Liberty Road
96	"	John Wadlow	20 Liberty Road
97	"	Samuel Harryman	16 Reisters Town
98	"	Charles & John Wethered	5 at the Franklin woolen works
99	"	Lewis C. Dugas	8 miles Liberty new cut Road
100	"	Wm Westerman	17 miles York road
101	"	Andrew Turner	30 York road
102	"	Elisha Carman	14 miles Joppa Road
103	"	Robert S. Hollins	5½ miles Falls turnpike
104	"	Levi Merryman	14 near York Road
105	"	Samuel Morton & Son	18 Oakland Factory
106	"	W^m & George Morris	8 miles Frederick (Thistle Factory)

[End of Original Page]

[6]

No.	Date	Name	Description	Amount
107	May 2	Peter Hoffman	34 miles old York Road	
108	" 19	John Davis	18 miles old Landing Road	$11.50
109	" 2	Samuel Cockey	11 Falls Road	
110	" "	Benjamin Buck & Son	15 old Phil^a Road	
111	" 24	Alexis Green	16 old York Road	$11.27
112	" 25	Nicholas Buckingham	25 Deer Park	$11.18
113	" 2^d	Wm Dwyer	14 Reisterstown road	
114	" 28	John Macklan	4 miles Falls road	$11.12½
115	" 2	John C. Jameson	6 miles Liberty road	
116	" 2	Henry Wier	26 York Road	
117	Jun 1	Charles Murden	18 miles Manor Road	$11.00
120	Jun 1	Jacob H. Minnickhyson	16 near Phil^a Road	$11.00
121	May 2	William Kelly	10 Fred^k Road	
122	" "	Solomon Allen	16 Liberty Road	
123	July 1	Andrew Hall	8 Falls Road	$10.00
124	" 7	John W. Ringrose	30 Fred^k Road	$9.83
125	May 2	John Stansbury	Hooks Town R^d	$12.00
126	July 14	Hugh Fox	30 Fred^k Road	$9.60
127	July 21	Caleb Bishop	13 miles Dover road	$9.37
128	Augt 1	Francis Fedemyer	8 Fred^k Road	$9.00
129	May 2	Jno. Clarke	12 York Road	$12.00
130	Augt 1	Leef John	15 Falls Road	$9.00
131	July 1	John Wonn	10 miles liberty road	$10.00
132	May 2	William Mallahein	19 Patapsco Falls	$12.00
133	Sep 29	John Jones	25 York Road	$7.66
134	" "	Peregrine Gorsuch	13 Reisters Town Road	$7.06
135	Oct 4	James Jones	3 Harford Road	$6.93
136	May 2	Samuel Phelps	27 near Fred^k Road	$12.00

[End of Original Page]

[7]

137	Oct 15	Darius Litzinger	9 Falls Road	$6.53
138	" 19	Joshua Brown	30 Fred^k Road	6.44
139	" 29	John Harryman	14 near Warren Factory	6.10
140	" "	Eli Scott	16 Falls Road	6.10
1831	Nov 1	George Beckley	24 old York road from 1^t May	$12.00
	" "	Thomas Galloway	11 Furnace Road from 1^t May	12.00
	" 2	Robert Ward	14 miles Liberty road from 1^t May	12.00
	" "	Edward Orrick	20 near York Road	5.97
	" 8	Wm T. Heston	19 near Reisters Town	5.75
	" 11	John Harker	6 Harford Road	5.67
	" 21	Warren C^o.	14 Warren Factory from 1^t May	12.00
	" 22	Jno. R. Gwynn	4 miles Falls road from 1^t May	12.00
	" 22	Joseph J. Walters	10 Liberty road from 1^t Nov Inst.	6.00
	" 24	Henry Rhodes	9 miles Fred^k Road from 2^d May	12.00
	" 28	Arabella Pierpoint	7 Fredk Road from 2^d May	12.00
	Dec 17	William Brooks	18 near York Road	4.50
	" 22	Charles Baker	15 Harford Road	4.31
1832				
	Jan 11	Daniel Anthony	10 Back River neck Road	3.70
	" 18	James Merford	12 York Road	3.47
	Feby 25	Benjamin Simpers	20 Falls Road	2.25
	Mar 13	Saml Sparhawk	18 near Sumwalts Mill	1.62½
	" 23	Ephraim Cox	23 York Road	1.31
	" 24	Hugh Downey	10 Ohio Rail Road	1.25
	" 29	Zacheas Durham	1¾ miles Falls Road	1.10
	Ap^L 5	Union Manftg Co.	10 Patapsco (from 2^d May Inst.)	12.00

[End of Original Page]

[19] Ordinary Licenses $18

May 1	John Little	Freedom 22 miles Liberty road
"	John Strickert	3 miles Bel Air road
"	Peter Blatchley	3 miles York road
"	John Wentz	33 miles Reisters Turnpike
"	Walter Martin	15 miles Harford Turnpike
"	John Burnham	13 miles Falls Turnpike
"	Mary Brookens	2½ miles, Philadelphia road
"	Ephraim Tipton	13 miles Falls Turnpike
"	Ja^s Willingham	3 miles Harford Turnpike
"	Danl Ferney	16 miles Reisters Turnpike
"	John Weaver of H^y	34 miles Hanover Turnpike
"	Henry Starr	1½ miles York Turnpike
"	Wm Allen	4 miles Phil^a Turnpike
"	Mary Mayzo	5 miles Trapp Turnpike
"	Saml Webb	16 miles Manor Turnpike
"	Joseph Sewell	1½ miles Harford Turnpike
"	Wm W. Riggen	2 miles York Turnpike
"	John Roberts	7 miles Frederick Turnpike
"	John G. Linsley	2½ miles Bel Air Turnpike
"	Catherine America	2½ miles Harford Turnpike
"	James Burton	12 miles Harford Turnpike
"	John King	8½ miles Reisters' Turnpike
"	Geo: Ilgenfritz	10 miles Reisters' Turnpike
"	George Fuller	6 miles Bel Air Turnpike
"	Eliz^a Stapleton	2 miles Phil^a Turnpike
"	Robert McCauley	6 miles Phil^a Turnpike
"	Jacob Worley	12 miles York road
"	Elisha Coe	8½ miles Back river road
"	Richard Paine	8 miles Back river road
"	Wm Jones	14 miles Middle river road
"	Thomas Arnold	5 miles Phil^a
"	Wm Gray	6½ miles Harford road
"	Adam Mungan	5½ miles Falls road
"	Fredk Brandt	2 miles Phil^a road
"	Elisha Battee	2 miles Bel Air
"	~~William Foon~~ William Hague	1¾ miles Harford road

[18] May 1 Francis Tress   4 miles Liberty road
"   John McMechen   9 miles Fred^k road
"   Thomas Wallace   7 miles York
"   ~~Joseph W. Miller~~ Charles Ford 5 miles Old Fred^k road
"   Jno Burk of Benjn   10 miles Phil^a road
"   Nich^s Leamon   2 miles Frederick road
"   Andrew McSherry 6½ miles Hookstown road
"   Edward Griffin   3 miles Hookstown road
"   Saml Walker   8½ York road
"   James Perigo   7 miles York road
"   Louis Larpenter   4 miles Reisters' road
"   John Farmer   3 miles Washington road
"   Jonathan Vanhorn   13½ Philadelphia road
"   Jacob Hartzell Jr.   14 miles Reisters' road
"   Patrick Mooney   9 miles Bel Air
"   Joseph Allison   4 miles York
"   Caleb Bishop   3¾ miles Harford road
"   John Roads   2¼ miles Annapolis road
"   Francis Feelemyer   6 miles Fred^k road
"   Wm Owings   7 miles Fred^k road
"   Jacob Stick   20 miles Hanover road
"   Benjn Garrett   24 miles York road
"   John Henshaw   8 miles Harford road
"   Garn^t Watkins   16 miles Harford road
"   Aquila Sparks   30 miles Old York road
"   Robt Woodward   1 mile near Canton
"   Levi Gibbs   7 miles Falls
"   Jo^s W. Stone   3 miles Frederick road
"   Lewis Robinson   2¾ miles Frederick road
"   Henry Carter   18 miles Liberty road
"   John W. Onion   15½ miles Phil^a road
"   John L. Sterns   8½ miles Frederick road
"   John Maxwell   2½ miles York road
"   Lloyd McAllister   7 miles Reisterstown road
"   Wm Moran   3½ York road

[End of Original Page]

[17] May 1	Francis Gray	9 miles Frederick road	
"	James Tongue	8 miles Frederick road	
"	Eliz^a Brookhart	14 miles Old York road	
"	Joseph Frost	5 miles Reisters town road	
"	Robert Ward	15 miles Liberty road	
"	Geo: Gelbach	2½ miles Old Harford	
"	John Fisher	16 miles Reisters' road	
"	Wm Thompson	28 miles Hanover road	
"	Ann Freburger	11 miles Back river road	
"	Peter House	5 miles Frederick road	
"	Levi Hoffman	3 miles Frederick road	
"	~~Peter G. H~~		
"	Zeney Linnard	four miles York road	
"	Saml Stubbins	17 miles York road	
"	Mary Pickett	4½ miles Hillens' road	
"	Martin Bowers	2 miles York	
"	William Slade	20 miles old York road	
"	David Kennedy	2 miles York	
"	George Barnett	8 miles new Liberty road	
"	Abraham Kuntz	24 Westminster road	~~not issued~~
"	Jacob Tayman	7 miles Hooks' town road	
"	Thomas Littlejohn	3 miles near Canton	
"	Wm Lewis Smith	9 miles Fredereick road	
"	Christ^n Cook	5 miles Liberty road	
"	~~Saml Morton & Son~~	~~18 miles Oakland Factory~~	
"	Peter Smyser	24 miles York road	
"	~~Alexis Green~~		
"	Andrew Cook	23 miles Liberty	
"	Acsah Buck	10 miles Harford	
"	Robt Ambrose	9 miles Falls road	
"	Thomas Craig	30 miles York road	
"	Wm Gamble	9 miles Frederick road	
"	Henry Rhoades	9 miles Frederick road	
"	George Hawkins	12 miles Havre de Grace road	

[End of Original Page]

[16] May 1   Benjn Kelly   Deer Park road 25 miles
     "   Joseph Bryan   22 miles on the Old York road
     "   Eliz^a Barthower   1½ new cut

1831 Ordinary Licenses

1	May 2	Samuel Harlan	2 miles Fred^k road	18
2	"	Peter Blatchley	3 miles York road	
3	"	Oliver Cromwell	3 miles Annapolis road	
4	"	Robert McCauley	6 miles Phil^a road	
5	"	Henry Starr	1½ miles York road	
6	"	Paul Rust	4½ miles Franklin road	
7	"	Charles Ford	5 miles Old Frederick road	
8	"	James Tongue	8 miles Frederick	
9	"	John Little	2½ miles Liberty	
10	"	Mary Mayzo	5 miles Trappe	
11	"	William Moon	1¾ miles Falls'	
12	"	Elizabeth Stapleton	2 miles Philadelphia	
13	"	Catharine Van Neukirk	2 miles Bel Air	
14	"	Elisha Coe	8½ miles near Phil^a road	
15	"	Israel Owings	11 miles new Liberty	
16	"	James Willingham	3 miles Harford	
17	"	Wesley Driver	8 miles Old Frederick	
18	"	Francis Herman Kaase	2 miles Philadelphia	
19	"	Samuel Owens	6½ miles Frederick	
20	"	Garrett Franklin	2¾ miles Bel Air	
21	"	Grace Mitchell	3¾ old Harford	
22	"	Thomas I. McCleary	6¾ Frederick	
23	"	John Milner	2 miles Reisters Town road	
24	"	Thomas J. Carter	18 miles Liberty road	
25	"	William S. Harrison	9 miles Fred^k road	
26	"	Elisha Battee	2 miles Bel Air road	
27	"	Francis Tress	4 miles Liberty road	
28	"	William Bacon	2 miles York road	
29	"	John King	8½ miles Reisters Town road	
30	"	Wm King	14 miles Reisters Town road	
31	"	Wm Slade	20 miles Old York road	

[End of Original Page]

[15] Ordinary Licenses Continued

32	May 2	Wm Jones	14 miles Middle river neck road
33	"	Levi Hoffman	3 miles Frederick road
34	"	Mary Brockam	2½ miles Phil^a road
31	"	George Mallonee	18 miles Falls road
32	"	Wm Hunter	30 miles Old York road
33	"	Peter Smyser	24 miles York turnpike
34	"	John Zouck	23 Falls Road
35	"	John Lemley	2½ miles Harford road
36	"	Ephraim Tipton	13 miles Falls turnpike
37	"	John Burnham	13 miles Falls turnpike
38	"	Jacob Stick	28 miles Hanover road
39	"	Samuel Webb	16 miles old York road
40	"	John Ertman	2½ miles Harford
41	"	Louis Larpenter	4 miles Reisters' Town road
42	"	Samuel Ulrich	30 miles old York
43	"	Saml Watkins	16 miles Harford
44	"	James McClure	14 miles Harford
	"	Nathan Rogers	
45	"	Otho Joseph Bryan	22 miles Old York
46	"	Richard Paine	8 miles Back river
47	"	James Walsh	1½ miles near Susquehanna railroad
48	"	Wm W. Riggin	1½ miles Harford road
49	"	James Perrigo	8 York Road
50	"	Leonard Keplinger	4 miles Phil^a Road
51	"	Nicholas Grimes	9 miles Middle river neck road
52	"	James Marsh	21 miles York
53	"	Thomas Parlett	11 miles Harford
54	"	Lloyd McAllister	7 miles Reisters' town road
55	"	John Wentz	33½ miles Balt Hanover road
56	"	George Showers	32½ miles Hanover road
57	"	Charles Miller	30½ miles Hanover road
58	"	George Baker	19½ miles Hanover road
59	"	Joshua Algire	22 miles Hanover road

[End of Original Page]

[14]   Ordinary Licenses Continued

60	May 2	Daniel Conn	20 miles York road
61	"	Adam Smyser	13½ miles York road
62	"	Daniel Ferney	16 miles Reisters town road
63	"	John Weaver	34 miles Reisters' town road
64	"	John Morrow	14 miles Reisters town road
65	"	Joseph Frost	5 miles same
66	"	Thomas Lewis	1½ Harford
67	"	Andrew Burk	23 miles Hanover road
~~68~~	"	~~John Bond~~	
68	"	Henry Null	24¾ miles Hanover
69	"	John Murray	2½ miles Philadelphia
70	"	Caleb Hunt	17 miles York
71	"	Samuel Stubbins	17 miles York
72	"	John Maxwell	2½ miles York
73	"	John Leaf	15 miles Falls' road
74	"	Thomas Wilson	3 miles York
75	"	Robert Woodward	1 mile near Canton
76	"	Lewis Bowen	9½ miles Falls
77	"	Peter House	5 miles Frederick
78	"	John G. Linsley	2½ miles Bel Air
79	"	Moses Parlett	9 miles old Harford
80	"	John Roads	2½ miles Annapolis road
81		Catharine Yeager	2 miles Falls
82	"	Nicholas Cornelius	10½ miles York
87	"	Abraham De Groff	7½ Fred^k road
88	"	Daniel Wiegant	1½ Rail Road
89	"	Lewis Robinson	3 Fred^k Road
90	"	Jacob Houck	34 Hanover Road
91	"	William L. Moran	3½ York Road
92	"	Charles Canoles	8 Harford
93	"	Joseph C. Jameson	6 miles Liberty
94	"	Wm Gray	6½ miles Harford
95	"	Eliz^a Brookhard	14 miles Old York
96	"	George Shealey	7 miles York
97	"	Nathan H. Ware	7 miles York
98	"	Daniel Freeland	7 miles York

[13] Ordinary Licenses Continued

99	May 2	Maria Eichelberger	4 miles, York road
100	"	Richard Hamilton	1 miles, York road
101	"	John Rutledge	21 York Road
102	"	Benjamin Garrett	23 York Road
103	"	Joseph Gardner	30 Hanover Road
104	"	David Hartzell	25 Westminster Road
105	"	George Batson	24½ Westminster Road
106	"	Jacob Hartzell	16 Reisters Town Road
~~107~~	"	~~William Ewing~~	~~24 Old York road~~
107	"	Henry Lamott	28 Hanover Road
108	"	Wm B. Gist	28 Hanover Road
109	"	George Fisher	16½ Reisters Town
110	"	William Horner	20 Westminster Road
111	"	Joshua Standiford	27 York Road
112	"	John R. Gwynn	4 miles Falls Road
113	"	Francis Gray	9 miles Frederick Road
114	"	William Gamble	9 miles Frederick Road
115	"	Joseph Allison	4 miles York Road
116	"	Wm Young	20 miles Westminster Road
117	"	Samuel Cable	22 miles same road
118	"	Elizabeth Dendy	1 mile York
119	"	Thomas Arnold	2 miles Washington
120	"	Joshua Crouse	4 miles York
121	"	Elizabeth Mumma	5 York
122	"	Christian Grove	14 Reisters Town Road
123	"	Jacob Worley	12 York Road
124	"	George Weaver	16¾ miles Reisters' town
125	"	Eliz^th Barthower	1½ miles new cut road
126	"	Ann Margaret Bowers	2 miles York
127	"	Christian Cook	5 miles Liberty
128	"	Caleb Bishop	3¾ miles Harford

[End of Original Page]

[12]   Ordinary Licenses Continued

No.	Date	Name	Location	Fee
129	May 2	Alexander Maydwell	1¼ Falls Road	
130	"	And^w McSherry	6½ miles Hooks town	
131	"	Wm Corbin	20 miles Westminster	
132	"	William Badders	13 miles Old York	
133	"	Janett Tipton	21 York Road	
134	"	Robert Ward	18 Liberty	
135	"	George Barnett	8 New Liberty	
136	" 4	Richard Bowers	3 Bel Air	$17.45
137	" 2	Saml Walker	8½ York	
138	"	Isaac Shoemaker	2½ Washington	
139	"	James Gibbs	1¼ miles Falls	
140	"	John Crist	22 miles Hanover	
141	"	John W. Onion	16 miles Philadelphia	
142	"	John Buck	10 Phila Road	
143	"	Charles Small	30 York Road	
144	"	George Hawkins	12 Havre de Grace	
145	"	Henry Rhodes	9 miles Frederick	
146	"	Dennis Davis	30 miles Hanover Road	
147	"	James F. Bonham	31 Fred^k Road	
148	"	Nicholas Lehman	2 Fred^k Road	
149	"	John Green	20 miles Liberty Road	
150	"	Edward Griffin	3 miles Reisters Town Road	
151	"	Francis Frelemyer	6½ Fred^k Road	
152	"	Lawrence Freed	33 miles Hanover Road	
153	" 2	Adam Mungan	5½ Falls Turnpike	
154	"	Andrew Smith	2 Washington Road	

[End of Original Page]

[11]

158	June 1	Philip Hannagan	4 Washington Road	$16.50
159	Jun 7	William Garey	16 Deer Park Road	16.25
160	" 20	Dennis Morrison	6 Falls	$15.55
161	May 2	John Lewin	4½ Reisters Town R^d	18.00
162	" 2	John Hanesworth	3 Washington Road	18.00
163	" 2	John Murphy	13 miles Reisters Town Road	$18.00
164	Jun 29	Henry Roatbaust	31 Hanover Road	$15.12
165	May 2	George Bishop	9 Harford Road	18.00
166	July 1	Solomon Conoway	10 Liberty Road	$15.00
167	May 2	John Conoway	25 Liberty Road	$18.00
168	July 1	Joseph Indik	10 Reisters Town Road	15.00
169	" 1	Philip Voltz	10 Liberty Road Ap^d	15.00
170	" 13	Patrick McGurk	30 Fred^k Road	14.40
171	June 1	John Lafferty	31 Fred^k Road	16.50
172	July 20	John Macklan	4 Falls Road	$14.05
173	July 26	Sarah Dillon	9 Fred^k Road	13.81
174	May 2	Joshua H. Kidd	5½ Miles Harford road	$18.00
175	" 2	Jno Clarke	12 York Road	18.00
176	Augt 5	Henry G. Brown	31 Rail Road	$13.37½
177	May 2	Catharine Bishop	10 Bel Air Road	$18.00
178	Augt 9	Solomon McHanney	26 Hanover Road	$13.18
179	" 12	Archibald Porter	16 Deer Park	13.00
180	" 23	John W. Ringrose	31 Fred^k Road	$12.37½
181	May 2	James Hartley	19 Liberty road	$18.00
182	Augt 24	~~Me~~ Isaac Marshall	30 Old York road	$12.40
183	June ~~26~~ 1	Moran Ann	4 Harford Road	$16.50
			S. Manning Esq. to pay	4.00
184	May 2	Elie Lilly	7 Liberty Road	$18.00

[End of Original Page]

[10] Ordinary Licenses

185	Augt 31	Jonathan Plowman	26 miles near York Road	$12.06
186	" 31	Henry Wier	26 miles near York Road	$12.06
187	May 2	Mary Pickett	4½ Hillens Road	$18.00
188	" "	Honour Woolry	25 Westminster road	$18.00
189	Sep 3	Samuel McCoy	15 Falls Road	$11.90
190	Sep 1	William McIlvaine	28 Hanover Road	$12.00
191	" 13	William Duncan	14½ near Warren Factory	11.50
192	" 16	Job Walter	6 old Fred^k Road	11.25
193	" 17	John R. Gwynn	4 Balt^o Susquehanna Road	11.20
194	May 2	Susan Pernie	9 Harford Road	18.00
195	Oct 4	James Jones	3 miles Harford Road	10.40
196	" 8	John Robertson	23 Westminster Road	10.20
197	" 7	John Roberts	7 Fredk Road	10.25
198	" 15	Darius Litzinger	9 Falls Road	$9.80
199	" 18	Wm A. Thompson	½ Canton White house	$9.70
200	" "	Michael Great	13 Reisters Town Road	$9.70
201	" 19	Charles Goddard	6½ Central race Course	9.65
202	" "	John Shipman	6½ Central race Course	9.65
203	" 20	James M. Selden	6½ Central race Course	9.60
204	" 21	Lewis Robinson	6½ Central race Course	9.55
205	" 22	Manoah Young	23 Liberty Road	9.50
206	" "	Horatio Miller	6½ Central race Course	9.50
207	May 2	Benjamin Kelly	26 Deer Park Road	$18.00
208	Oct 24	Theron Barnum	6½ Central race Course	$9.40
209	" "	Martin Weble	6 near Central Course	$9.40
210	" 18	Elias Woods	27½ Hooks Town Road	9.70
211	May 2	Elizabeth Conn	14 miles Reisters Town Road	$18.00

[End of Original Page]

[9] 1831

212	Oct 31	Benjamin F. Forester	32 Ohio Rail Road	$9.05
213	May 2	Gordon Bigham	4½ Liberty Road	18.00
214	Oct 31	Peter Storm	16 Reisters Town Road	9.05

1831

Nov 1	Thomas Galloway	11 Furnace Road from 1ᵗ May	$18.00
" 1	Jacob Tayman	7 Reisters Town Road from 1ᵗ May	18.00
" 2	Abraham King	14 Bel Air Road from 1ᵗ May	18.00
" 5	Jonathan M. Wilson	15 Warren Factory	8.80
" 7	James Cullimore	1¼ Harford Road	8.75
" 10	John Elder	24 Rail road	8.56
" 11	John Harker	6 Harford Road	8.50
" 16	Joshua Cross	14 near Warren Factory	8.25
" 18	John Hively	26 Hanover Road from 1ˢᵗ May	18.00
" 23	John Lamott	26 Falls Road	7.90
" 25	Wᵐ Crumrine	30 Hanover Road	7.80
Decʳ 7	Robert Alder	18 Dover Road	7.25
" 14	Wᵐ Phipps	2 York Road	6.90
" 14	Jesse Marshall	30 Old York Road	6.90
" 15	Peter Earbaugh	25½ Westminster Road	6.85
" 16	George Waller	18 Middle River Neck	6.80
" 19	William Carr	7 Fredᵏ Road	6.65
" 21	Conrad Ziagler	1½ Fredᵏ Road	6.55
" 24	David Musselman	24 Hanover Road	6.40
Jany 2	Samuel B. Hugo	2½ Bel Air road	6.00
" 9	James Campbell	2 Washington Road	5.65
Feby 8	James Curley	3 Washington Road	4.10
" 27	Joshua Oram	37 Ohio Rail road	3.15
March 6	Thomas S. Hamlin	Fredᵏ Roard ~~206.57~~	2.81
" 15	Charles Carnan	12¼ Philᵃ Road	2.37
" 23	Owen Elder	27 Ohio Rail road	2.00
" 29	Zacheas Durham	1¾ Falls Road	1.65
Apˡ 3	Joseph Wheeler	5½ Harford	1.40
" "	Jacob Frick	30 Hanover	1.40

[End of Original Page]

[8] 1832

April 4	Jacob Taney	24 Westminster Road	$1.37½
" 4	John Hardy	6 Fred^k Road	1.35
" 4	John Adams	31½ Fred^k Road	1.35
Ap^l 6	David Everhart	30½ Manchester	1.25
" 14	Cornelius McCann	1½ Susquehanna Rail Road	.87½

[End of Original Page]

Baltimore County Boundaries

In 1831, Baltimore County encompassed significantly more territory than it does today. Just six years later, in 1837, Carroll County was created from the western portion of Baltimore County and the eastern portion of Frederick County. Formerly, the town of Mt. Airy lay in the far southwest corner of Baltimore County. The old boundary between Frederick and Baltimore Counties ran approximately along Route 27 from Mt. Airy to Westminster, the seat of the new Carroll County straddling the old boundary, then headed more or less north to the Mason Dixon Line. The eastern boundary with Harford County has not changed, nor has the southwestern boundary with Anne Arundel County, except that Howard County was part of Anne Arundel County before 1851.

In 1830, the municipal boundaries of Baltimore City were significantly different than they are today. The eastern city boundary ran from north to south approximately along what then was called East Avenue, from the northeast corner of Baltimore Cemetery, south to the harbor, about where Decker Avenue runs today. The northern boundary ran along North Avenue, from Payson Street on the west to Baltimore Cemetery on the east. The western boundary was a diagonal line starting from North Avenue and Payson Street running nearly south southwest to where the old Baltimore and Ohio Railroad crossed the Gwynns Falls. The southern boundary followed the Gwynns Falls downstream to its confluence with Middle Branch.

License Fees and Terms

In 1830 and 1831, a trader license cost $12, more than the average monthly wage for farm labor, $10 including board, not an insignificant sum at that time. Based upon a comparison of average wage rates for production labor, the license fee is equivalent to more than $3,100 today. In 1830, forty-eight licensees paid the full $12 effective May 1st, only Samuel Choate of Reisterstown paying less, $11.30 for his license effective May 22. In 1831, one hundred eighteen licensees paid the full fee effective May 2, the first one hundred seven licensees listed together in a group. The next licensee, John Davis on Old Landing Road, paid the prorated amount of $11.50 effective May 19, implying that his business started on that date. The next licensee, Samuel Cockey on the Falls Road, paid the full amount effective May 2, implying that he was two weeks or so late in paying the fee. Benjamin Buck & Son on the Old Philadelphia Road, the next license entry, also paid the full amount effective May 2, evidently late as well. In all, one hundred eighteen licensees paid the full amount in 1831, nineteen of them evidently paying late.

The remaining twenty-two traders paid a smaller license fee, proportional to the remaining term of their license. For example, Charles Murden on Manor Road was licensed June 1, paying $11 for one less month. Similarly, John Harker on the Harford Turnpike paid the smallest fee, $5.67 effective November 11. The smaller, prorated fees, all with effective dates after May 1 or 2, imply that the licensees were just starting their trading businesses rather than paying their license fees late. From November 1, 1831 through April 5, 1832, no less than eight licensees paid the full $12 fee, all having the notation effective from May 1. During the same period, thirteen licensees each paid a smaller prorated amount. From the foregoing, it is evident that the term of each license was from May 1 through April 30 of the next year, not the calendar year, perhaps as the casual reader would assume. While eight licenses were issued in calendar year 1832, all were for 1831 licenses, seven for trading businesses started in the last months of the license year and one to the Union Manufacturing Company, who was very late in paying the required fee.

Three names, Elizabeth Young, George Gelbach, and Chainey Brooks, first were entered and then crossed out by the clerk, indicating that no license was issued and no fee was paid and implying that the individuals had sold or otherwise disposed of their businesses the previous year. No residence was entered for either Elizabeth Young or Chainey Brooks. James Perrigo was crossed out at Mile Post 7, but re-entered at Mile Post 8.

An ordinary license cost $18, an even more significant sum, equivalent to more than $4,700 today. Again, every licensee recorded on May 1 or 2 paid the full amount, those recorded on later dates paying a smaller prorated fee. In 1830, one hundred five licensees paid the full fee, all effective May 1 or 2, no one paying a smaller prorated fee with a later effective date. In 1831, the first one hundred thirty-five licensees paid the full fee effective May 1 or 2. The next licensee, Richard Bowers on the Bel Air Turnpike, paid $17.45 effective May 14, implying the effective date of his business. The next eighteen licensees paid the full amount, suggesting they were late in paying their fees. From June 15, 1831 through April 14, 1832, ninety-four licenses were issued, seventeen paying the full amount effective from May 1 or 2, 1831, the remaining seventy-seven paying smaller prorated amounts for later effective dates.

The name Joseph W. Miller was crossed out and the name Charles Ford entered on the same line at Mile Post 5 on Old Frederick Road, perhaps indicating that Charles Ford operated a tavern leased from Joseph Miller. Next to the entry for Abraham Kuntz, licensed at Mile Post 24 on the Westminster Turnpike, the clerk wrote "not issued," but later crossed out the two words, implying that the license indeed was issued. Five entries, Samuel Morton & Son, Alexis Green, Nathan Rogers, John Bond, and William Ewing, were crossed out by the clerk, indicating that no license was issued. The notation Ap^d in the entry for Philip Voltz possibly indicates that the license application remained open for some time before finally getting issued. Why the clerk noted that S. Manning, Esq. was to pay $4 is uncertain, his location in the ledger possibly indicating some relationship to the entry for Ann Moran. Thomas Galloway, Jacob Tayman, Abraham King, and John Hively, apparently were late in renewing their licenses.

It is curious that in 1830 only one trader license and no ordinary license was issued on a prorated basis; while in 1831 nineteen trader and seventy-seven ordinary licenses were prorated. One explanation for the glaring inconsistency could be that license enforcement was lax in 1830 and more stringent in 1831. In 1830, the clerk simply may have issued licenses only to those applicants who voluntarily came to the courthouse and, in 1831, realizing that significant noncompliance reduced revenue, began traveling the turnpikes and major roads looking for unlicensed businesses, perhaps explaining the absence of ordinary licenses in Highlandtown as well as in the small towns and villages not situated along the turnpikes, such as Beckleysville, Gorsuch Mills, Granite, Stablersville, Union Meeting House, and Woodberry.

Turnpikes and Taverns

Any understanding of the tavern keepers during the first half of the nineteenth century in Baltimore County requires an understanding of the turnpikes on which the vast majority of the establishments were dependent, taverns and turnpikes inextricably linked by geography, commerce, tradition, and folk lore.

In 1787, the state legislature authorized five turnpikes in Baltimore County: the first from Baltimore to Frederick, the second from Baltimore to Reisterstown, the third from Reisterstown to Westminster, the fourth from Reisterstown to Hanover, and the fifth from Baltimore to York, the construction and subsequent management of the turnpikes entrusted to county officials. The scheme for turnpiking under county authority largely was unsuccessful; the 1787 law amended no less than ten times in the first fourteen years. By 1802, fifteen years later, only the Reisterstown Turnpike was complete and all five were running deficits. In 1804-5, the legislature privatized the turnpike system by creating three companies: one for the Baltimore and Frederick Town Turnpike Road; the second for the Baltimore and Reisterstown Turnpike Road, including the Reisterstown, Hanover, and Westminster Turnpikes; and, the third for the Baltimore and York Town Turnpike Road. The Falls Turnpike Company was incorporated the same year by different legislation. The previously unsuccessful Baltimore and Washington Turnpike Company of 1796 was replaced by a new company in 1812 to construct a turnpike from Baltimore to Norwood's Ferry on the Patapsco River, then by McCoy's Tavern, Vansville, the White House, Ross' Tavern, and Blandensburg, to Washington. In 1813, still another company was authorized to construct the Baltimore and Havre de Grace Turnpike.[3]

As the various turnpikes reached their destinations, traffic increased substantially to and from Baltimore. York County farmers realized

---

[3] Maryland Geological Survey, *Report on the Highways of Maryland*. The Johns Hopkins University Press, Baltimore, Maryland, 1899.

the markets in Baltimore were half the distance to Philadelphia and farmers in Adams County were even more favorably situated. When the last section of turnpike was completed to Cumberland, the National Road opened Ohio to the Baltimore markets. Over the turnpikes a stream of wealth rolled into Baltimore, the nearest market to the western country in the first half of the nineteenth century. During the first three decades of the century, the population of Baltimore grew fivefold, faster than any other city in the country. Large quantities of livestock, flour, whiskey, butter, and other agricultural products were transported to Baltimore for shipment, the turnpikes linking the products of a vast portion of Ohio, Kentucky, Pennsylvania, and Maryland with the outside world. In 1827, one gentleman traveling on the turnpike between Baltimore and Frederick, counted 235 wagons, almost seven per mile, each very large in size and heavily loaded. The production, including flour and cotton, manufactured by the mills and factories along the Patapsco River, Gwynns Falls, Jones Falls, and Gunpowder Rivers, made its way to the Baltimore markets by way of the turnpikes.[4]

The turnpike traffic spurred the growth of three distinct classes of taverns to serve the throng of travelers. The taverns where stage horses were kept and exchanged were called stage houses, often located at twelve-mile intervals, offering both meals and overnight accommodations. Usually considered to be of the highest class, stage houses served politicians going to and from their capitals, judges and attorneys attending courts, country merchants, foreign travelers, and affluent emigrants, whether traveling by stagecoach or private means. The great majority of taverns were called wagon stands, catering mostly to wagoners as well as the less affluent travelers, each stand providing a wagon yard where teams were driven to feed and rest overnight and within the tavern a bar where refreshments were served. After an evening of merriment, most of the wagoners rolled out their beds on the bar room floor. The third class of taverns, catering

---

[4] Durrenburger, Joseph Austin, *Turnpikes, A Study of the Toll Road Movement in the Middle Atlantic States and Maryland.* John E. Edwards, Publisher, Cos Cob, Connecticut, 1968.

mostly to drovers, generally was situated outside of towns and villages where lodging and food for the drovers and pasture, water, and feed for the droves were provided. It was not uncommon for taverns to offer services of blacksmiths, wheelwrights, coopers, harness makers, and other craftsmen.

Tabulation

The following tables place each licensee along their road in order by mile post, noting the license year and the approximate location relative to a modern landmark, usually the name of a nearby intersecting street, but sometimes a town, river, cemetery, or other feature. Many readers will recognize the names of the roads and turnpikes in the two lists, virtually all of which continue today. Most of the roads cited in the original records began in or near the city, radiating outward like the spokes of a wheel, most of the modern roads generally following the alignments of the old roads and turnpikes. Over the past eighteen decades or so, the names of many streets have changed; for example, the numbered streets and avenues in Canton have been replaced with such names as Boston, Cardiff, Haven, and Holabird. Moreover, as transportation and development demands have changed, old roads have been moved, widened, straightened, and sometimes even totally obliterated, all in the name of progress, making it difficult, if not impossible, to pinpoint a particular mile post along a road alignment that no longer exists.

The vast majority of the traders and ordinaries were licensed at a particular mile post, probably no more accurately than say plus or minus one half mile or so. The ordinaries, of course, were situated right along the road; but, the traders may have resided or done business elsewhere. Most traders probably were licensed at their residences and conducted their businesses from there; however, at least some were licensed at their mill or factory and resided elsewhere. Several licenses were issued at a particular mile post and a half, probably no more accurately than more or less midway between mile posts. Those few licensed at a mile post and one quarter or three quarters, in a similar manner, probably no more accurately than closer to one mile post than the other.

The table for each turnpike or major road is presented starting with the Annapolis Road to the south, proceeding in a more or less clockwise fashion to the Middle River Neck Road on the southeast. Following each table, a brief history and description of the old roadway alignment as well as differences between the old and new routes and alignments are presented. Curiosities, errors, and other anomalies discovered during the analysis of the license lists are presented. In addition, business interests are identified and located and a few simple statistics are noted. After the turnpikes and major roads, the remaining persons licensed at relatively scattered places are located relative to modern landmarks.

Based upon the results of the tabulation, it is evident that the mile posts represent distances along the turnpikes. For the remaining roads and other locations, the mile posts apparently represent straight line distances from the courthouse then in Baltimore City, almost as if the clerk drew concentric circles around the courthouse at one-mile intervals on his map and asked each licensee to locate his residence or place of business relative to the circles. Moreover, all of the licensees were located outside of the city, the incorporated municipality apparently licensed ordinaries and traders separately.

Annapolis Road

Mile Post	Licensee	Year	Approximate Location
2¼	John Roads	1830	Waterview Avenue
2½	John Roads	1831	Waterview Avenue
3	Oliver Cromwell	1831	Patapsco Avenue

Today, the Annapolis Road begins in the city at the intersection of Russell and Bush Streets and proceeds in a southerly direction to the Patapsco River, the Anne Arundel County boundary, about Mile Post 4½. Only about one and one half miles of the Annapolis Road lies within the county today. The old Annapolis Road began at a point that then was in the county at about Mile Post 2½, near the modern intersection of Annapolis Road, Waterview Avenue, and Russell Street and generally followed the alignment of the modern road. John Roads probably did not move his ordinary from year to year, more likely his description of the location changed. No traders were licensed along Annapolis Road. Only two ordinaries were licensed along Annapolis Road, none to women, averaging one ordinary per mile. The Annapolis Road was not operated as a turnpike.

Washington Turnpike

Mile Post	Licensee	Year	Approximate Location
2	Andrew Smith	1830	Gwynns Falls
2	Thomas Arnold	1830	Gwynns Falls
2	James Campbell	1831	Gwynns Falls
2	John M. Wheat	1831	Gwynns Falls
2½	Isaac Shoemaker	1830	Hollins Ferry Road
3	James Curley	1831	Desoto Road
3	John Farmer	1830	Desoto Road
3	John Hanesworth	1830	Desoto Road
4	Philip Hannagan	1830	Lansdowne Road

The Washington and Baltimore Turnpike Road Company was chartered in 1812 with capital of $100,000.[5] Milestones were erected along the gravel road, giving the distance to Baltimore, but not to Washington, the last surviving milestone in Beltsville. A tollgate was just north of the Gwynns Falls, near Carroll Park Golf Course.

---

[5] Hollifield, William, *Difficulties Made Easy, History of the Turnpikes of Baltimore City and County*, Page 13. Baltimore County Historical Society, Cockeysville, Maryland, 1978. (Hereinafter cited as Hollifield.)

The original turnpike began in the city heading west along Pratt Street, just east of Mount Clare Station turning south, proceeding in a southwesterly direction, generally following present-day Washington Avenue, crossing the city boundary into the county at the Gwynns Falls about Mile Post 2½ and crossing the Patapsco River into Anne Arundel County near Mile Post 7. Mile Post 2 actually was close to present-day Monroe Street; however, because Mile Post 2 was in the city, the four men licensed at that mile post probably were located just to the west of the Gwynns Falls in the county, supported by the fact that no men with those names are listed as either tavern keepers, traders, or other similar occupations in the 1829 or 1833 city directories.[6] Only one trader, John M. Wheat, was licensed on the Washington Turnpike. No business concerns or women were licensed. With eight ordinaries licensed, the Washington Turnpike averaged one ordinary about every three quarters of a mile.

---

[6] *Matchett's Baltimore Directory, 1829 and 1833.* Maryland State Archives, Annapolis, Maryland.

Baltimore and Ohio Railroad

Mile Post	Licensee	Year	Approximate Location
10	Hugh Downey	1832	Patapsco State Park
13	Saib Devries	1831	Granite
27	Owen Elder	1831	Woodbine Road
32	Benjamin F. Forester	1831	Mount Airy
37	Joshua Oram	1831	Mount Airy (?)

Four licenses were issued to traders situated on the Ohio Railroad, no doubt the Baltimore and Ohio Railroad, the main line beginning at Camden Yards, heading southwest, crossing the Gwynns Falls near Mile Post 1, crossing Hammonds Ferry Road near Mile Post 4, crossing the Washington Turnpike at Mile Post 6, crossing the Patapsco River at Mile Post 7, following the Patapsco River to Marriottsville near Mile Post 15, and following the West Branch of Patapsco River to Mount Airy at Mile Post 31, before heading to Harpers Ferry and points west.

Hugh Downey was licensed at Mile Post 10, probably at or near Wrights Mill, now in Patapsco Valley State Park, near Wrights Mill Road. Saib Devries was licensed as a trader at Mile Post 13, near the Baltimore and Ohio Railroad, probably at or near the village of Granite, about one mile north of the railroad. Joshua Oram was licensed a Mile Post 37, well into Frederick County, south of Frederick in the vicinity of the Monocracy River crossing, indicating an error in the mile post. The three licensed ordinaries probably were closer to the railroad than to the Frederick Turnpike, implying they depended upon railroad workers for clientele. In 1831, John Elder was licensed for an ordinary at Mile Post 24 on the Rail Road, but which railroad not recorded by the clerk. If his ordinary was located on the Baltimore and Ohio Railroad, Mile Post 24 is close to the Hoods Mill Road crossing, about four miles southwest of Eldersburg.

Frederick Turnpike

Mile Post	Licensee	Year	Approximate Location
1½	Conrad Ziagler	1831	South Bentalou Street
2	Nicholas Leamon	1830, 1831	Franklintown Road
2	Samuel Harlan	1831	Franklintown Road
2¾	Lewis Robertson	1830	Gwynns Falls
3	Aquila Jarvis	1830	3377 Frederick Avenue
3	John W. Stone	1830	3377 Frederick Avenue
3	Levi Hoffman	1830, 1831	3377 Frederick Avenue
5	Charles Ford	1831	McCurley Street
5	Peter House	1830, 1831	National Cemetery
6	Francis Feelemyer	1830, 1831	Delray Avenue
6	Job Walter	1831	Ingleside Avenue
6	John Hardy	1832	Delray Avenue
6½	Samuel Owens	1831	Melvin Avenue
6¾	Thomas I. McCleary	1831	Wyndcrest Avenue
7	John Roberts	1830, 1831	South Rolling Road

Mile Post	Licensee	Year	Approximate Location
7	William Carr	1831	South Rolling Road
7	William Owings	1830	South Rolling Road
7	Arabella Pierpoint	1831	South Rolling Road
7½	Abraham De Groff	1831	North Rolling Road
8	Charity Thompson	1830	Thistle Road
8	James Tongue	1830, 1831	Thistle Road
8	William & George Morris	1831	Thistle Road
8	Wesley Driver	1831	Edmondson Avenue
8	Francis Fedemyer	1831	Thistle Road
8½	John L. Sterns	1830	Old Frederick Road
9	John McMechen	1830	Ellicott City
9	Francis Gray	1830, 1831	Ellicott City
9	William Lewis Smith	1830	Ellicott City
9	William Gamble	1830, 1831	Ellicott City
9	Henry Rhodes	1830, 1831	Ellicott City
9	William Harrison	1831	Ellicott City

Mile Post	Licensee	Year	Approximate Location
9	Sarah Dillon	1831	Ellicott City
9½	Edward Gray	1830, 1831	Ellicott City

Through much of the twentieth century, the primary road from Baltimore to Frederick was known as the Baltimore National Pike, designated US Route 40. In earlier times, there were three different routes to Frederick within Baltimore County, each in turn known as Frederick Road in their day. The first Frederick Road was built in the 1760s by German settlers desiring a means to get their crops to the wider market in Baltimore. Much of the original route exists today, crossing over the Patapsco River into Baltimore County from the west just north of I-70, following Johnnycake Road from Hollofield Road eastward to the Baltimore National Pike, and following Old Frederick Road to its end at the intersection of Frederick Avenue, Hilton Street, and Caton Avenue.[7] By 1830, the original route had been superseded twice, no longer a viable route to market.

Starting in 1771, the Ellicott brothers, Joseph, Andrew, and John, established Ellicott's Lower Mills, at a place on the Patapsco River called "The Hollow" about ten miles west of Baltimore, now the site of Ellicott City. Needing a convenient route to transport their product to market, Ellicott & Company built a new road east to Baltimore called Ellicott's Mills Road by circa 1787. The name Ellicott's Mills Road gradually changed to Frederick Road as the

---

[7] Hainesworth, Lorna, *Difficulties Made Easy, History of Travel Routes Between Frederick and Maryland.* Lornament Press, Randallstown, Maryland, 2012. (Hereinafter cited as Hainesworth.)

Ellicotts built a new road west eventually connecting Baltimore to Frederick.[8] That second Frederick Road, now called Old Frederick Road, begins at Hilton Street and then heads in a northwesterly direction until it intersects Edmondson Avenue at Glen Allen Drive. The old road picks up just west of the Beltway, parallels the Baltimore National Pike one block to the south, and dead ends just before Rolling Road. The old road picks up again about two blocks south on Rolling Road, heads in a southwesterly direction, and merges back into Frederick Road about one half mile from Ellicott City and the Howard County boundary.

Jonathan Ellicott became the first president of the Baltimore Frederick Turnpike Company in 1805. The first Frederick Turnpike, constructed circa 1805 to 1808, generally follows present-day Frederick Avenue in the city and Frederick Road in the county, from its beginning at the corner of West Baltimore and South Gilmor Streets, heading in a southwesterly direction, to the old city boundary at West Pratt Street, just past Mile Post 2, past Mount Olivet Cemetery near Mile Post 3, heading in a westerly direction through Catonsville about Mile Post 6½, and ending at the crossing of the North Branch of the Patapsco River at Mile Post 9½, near Ellicott City. One tollgate was located adjacent to Mount Olivet Cemetery, another at Catonsville, and a third between Ellicott City and the intersection with Old Frederick Road.

Six of the original milestones in old Baltimore County survive today, although two apparently are not in their original location.[9] Mile Stone 3 is on the north side in front of an old church at 3377 Frederick Avenue, between McCurley and Hilton Streets, the former site of the

---

[8] Hainesworth.

[9] Harlowe, Jerry L., *Mile Markers of the Baltimore and Frederick-Town Turnpike, 1805-2005.* Patapsco Falls Press, Catonsville, Maryland, 2005.

Fairview Inn, possibly operated by one of those licensed at that location.

Fairview Inn[10]

Mile Stone 4 is on the north side opposite 4513 Frederick Avenue, just east of Beechfield Avenue. Mile Stone 5 sits next to the entrance of the National Cemetery, probably not in its original position as it is the only milestone on the south side of the former turnpike. Mile Stone 6, showing the distance to Baltimore, is located on the north side of Frederick Road near Delray Avenue. Mile Stone 7 was located just west of Beechwood Avenue; but, now is on the grounds of the Catonsville Public Library, where it was relocated in 1963. Mile Stone 9 is located on the north side of the old turnpike, just west of the house numbered 2716, Gray's Level, near the so-called Devil's Elbow.[11] Mile Stone 10 is just inside Howard County underneath the railroad crossing at the entrance to Ellicott City.

---

[10] Courtesy of the Enoch Pratt Free Library, Baltimore, Maryland.

[11] Inventory of Historic Properties, BA-2459, 2460, and 2461. Maryland Historical Trust, Annapolis, Maryland.

The original turnpike crossed the city boundary into the county at South Bentalou Street, about Mile Post 2¼. Three men, Conrad Ziagler, Nicholas Leamon, and Samuel Harlan, all licensed at mile posts implying locations within the city limits, more probably were located along the turnpike between South Bentalou Street and the Gwynns Falls. While certainly not conclusive, none of the three men appear in the city directories in 1829 or 1833.

In the 1830s, the first wagon stand west of Baltimore was kept by a man named Hawes, seven miles from the city, wagoners often leaving in the morning, driving to Baltimore, unloading and reloading, returning to it in the evening of the same day, and leaving it the next morning on their journey west. The Hawes Tavern ceased to operate in 1840.[12] Perhaps one of the licensees located in Catonsville operated the Hawes Tavern in 1831.

Lewis Robertson was licensed at Mile Post 2¾ in 1830 and Lewis Robinson was licensed at Mile Post 3 in 1831, very probably the same man. Thomas S. Hamlin was licensed on Frederick Road; but, no mile post was recorded, making it impossible to locate the man along the turnpike. William Owings, Samuel Harlan, Samuel Owens, Charles Ford, and Henry Rhodes were licensed both as ordinaries and as traders. William and George Morris, apparently a business interest, was licensed as a trader at Mile Post 8, with the notation Thistle Factory, one of only two mills still operating in the Patapsco valley and the only one containing portions of the original building. Alexander Fridge and William Morris purchased the property at Ilchester from the Ellicott family in 1823 and began construction of a cotton mill the following year. During construction, Fridge sold his

---

[12] Searight, Thomas B., *The Old Pike*. The original edition of 1894 edited by Joseph E. Moorse and R. Duff Green and published by Green Tree Press, Orange, Virginia, 1971.

half interest to George Morris of Philadelphia. The Thistle Manufacturing Company was incorporated by the General Assembly in 1834.[13] The old mill is located at the southern end of Thistle Road about one mile from the old turnpike, an indication of the approximate nature of the mile post locations.

Mile Stone 31 is located on the north side of the old turnpike, now East Ridgeville Boulevard, just east of Ridgeside Drive, within the municipal limits of Mount Airy.[14] Four distant trader licenses were issued in 1831, to Samuel Phelps near Mile Post 27 and to John W. Ringrose, Hugh Fox, and Joshua Brown, all at Mile Post 30, in the vicinity of Mount Airy, a portion of which then was in Baltimore County, but placed into Carroll County in 1837. Five distant ordinary licenses were issued to Patrick McGurk at Mile Post 30, to James F. Bonham, John Lafferty, and John W. Ringrose at Mile Post 31, and to John Adams at Mile Post 31½, in the vicinity of Mount Airy.

Francis Feelemyer was licensed as an ordinary promptly at the start of each license year, at Mile Post 6 in 1830 and at Mile Post 6½ in 1831, possibly indicating a move from one tavern stand to another in Randallstown, but more probably indicating a more precise later description. Francis Fedemyer, probably the same man supplementing his income, was licensed as a trader effective August 1, 1831 at Mile Post 8 near the various mills at Ellicott City.

---

[13] Inventory of Historic Properties, BA-144. Maryland Historical Trust, Annapolis, Maryland.

[14] Inventory of Historic Properties, CR-662. Maryland Historical Trust, Annapolis, Maryland.

Charles Ford at Mile Post 5, Job Walter at Mile Post 6, and Wesley Driver at Mile Post 8 were licensed on old Frederick Road, their approximate locations in the table relative to the Old Frederick Road. In 1830 and 1831, Wright & Bailey were licensed as traders at Mile Post 13 near old Frederick Road, a mile post clearly then past Ellicott City in  Anne Arundel County but now in Howard County, perhaps situated at Granite, about two miles north of the old turnpike, across the river in Baltimore County.

All, but one of the thirty-three licenses, were issued to individuals, three to women and twenty-nine to men. Twenty-nine ordinaries were licensed between the city boundary and Ellicott City, an average of one ordinary every quarter mile.

MileStone 3

Mile Stone 10

Liberty Road

Mile Post	Licensee	Year	Approximate Location
4	Francis Tress	1830, 1831	Hilton Street
4½	Gordon Bigham	1831	Ayrdale Avenue
5	Christian Cook	1830, 1831	Granada Avenue
6	Joseph C. Jameson	1831	Rogers Avenue
7	Elie Lilly	1831	Woodlawn Cemetery
8	Lewis C. Dugas	1831	Fairview Road
8	Geoge Barnett	1830, 1831	Fairview Road
10	Joseph J. Walters	1831	Clifmar Road
10	John Wonn	1831	Clifmar Road
10	Philip Voltz	1831	Clifmar Road
10	Sarah Allen	1830	Clifmar Road
10	Solomon Conoway	1831	Clifmar Road
11	Israel Owings	1831	Briarstone Road
12	Samuel Penny	1831	Chapman Road
14	Robert Ward	1831	Herrara Court

Mile Post	Licensee	Year	Approximate Location
14	Sarah Allen	1831	Herrara Court
14	Larkin Young	1830	Herrara Court
15	Robert Ward	1830, 1831	Allen Road
16	Solomon Allen	1831	Liberty Ridge Court
18	William Garey	1830	North Branch
18	Henry Carter	1830	North Branch
18	Thomas J. Carter	1831	North Branch
19	James Hartley	1831	Marvin Avenue
20	John Wadlow	1831	Georgetown Boulevard
20	Catherine Chambers	1831	Georgetown Boulevard
20	John Ware	1830, 1831	Georgetown Boulevard
20	Otho Shipley	1830, 1831	Georgetown Boulevard
20	John Green	1831	Georgetown Boulevard
22	John Little	1830, 1831	Freedom
23	Andrew Cook	1830	Dorseys Crossroads
23	Manoah Young	1831	Dorseys Crossroads

Mile Post	Licensee	Year	Approximate Location
25	John Conoway	1831	Old Washington Road

In 1843, residents petitioned the state legislature to charter a turnpike company, noting the old Liberty Road was in deplorable condition, impassable for a large portion of the year. In 1866, soon after the turnpike was completed, a local newspaper described the turnpike as efficiently managed and prosperous, having introduced many improvements into a section of the county *"previously very backward on account of bad roads."*[15] Because the alignment of Liberty Road before the turnpike is uncertain, the locations in the foregoing table assume the old road substantially followed is current alignment. The southern end of the old Liberty Road intersected the Hookstown Turnpike near Mile Post 3, now the intersection of Liberty Heights Avenue and Reisterstown Road near Mondawmin. The road proceeded more or less in a straight line in a northwesterly direction through Randallstown and Eldersburg to the old boundary with Frederick County near Winfield at Mile Post 25.

The residence of Doctor Joseph W. Steele, in the village of Freedom, a log weather-boarded structure built about 1769, operated as a tavern since the Revolution. John Little owned the tavern for many years.[16]

George Barnett at Mile Post 8 and Israel Owings at Mile Post 11, were licensed on "new Liberty Road," the significance of the adjective "new" now lost to history. Similarly, William Barnett at Mile Post 7 and Samuel Penny at Mile Post 12 were licensed on Old Liberty;

---

[15] Hollifield, Page 28.

[16] J. Thomas Scharf, *History of Western Maryland*, Volume II, Page 877. Louis H. Everts, Philadelphia, Pennsylvania, 1882. (Hereinafter cited as Scharf.)

however, no evidence has been found of any realignments of the old road before 1831 on available maps. Lewis C. Dugas was licensed at Mile Post 8 on Liberty new cut Road, the meaning of the words "new cut" also now lost to history.

Beale Buckingham was licensed at Mile Post 31 on Liberty Road, approximately six miles west of Winfield, across the boundary into what then was Frederick County, indicating an error in recording either the mile post, road name, or both. John Ware was licensed as a trader at Mile Post 2 on Liberty Road and as an ordinary at Mile Post 20 near Eldersburg. Because Liberty Road began at Mile Post 3, John Ware's trader license probably was located near Mile Post 20 at Eldersburg. William Odell was licensed at Mile Post 15 near Liberty Road, probably on or near Powell's Run Road. Sarah Allen was licensed at Mile Post 10 in 1830 and at Mile Post 14 in 1831, apparently having moved her trading business from the vicinity of Old Court Road to Holbrook.

Ward's New Tavern[17]

The New Tavern was located on the north side of the Liberty Road, just east of Wards Chapel Road in Holbrook, now 10918 Liberty Road.[18] The New Tavern, built by Robert Ward in 1802, also served the Methodists, who held their services there until 1845. Samuel Penny may have owned the Harrison Hotel on the corner of Liberty Road and Marriottsville Road, between Mile Posts 12 and 13, the old hotel torn down in 1973.[19]

Now known as the Choate House, the old tavern built by Michael Riddlemoser circa 1810 at the present-day address of 9600 Liberty Road in Randallstown, is located between Mile Posts 11 and 12. The property was purchased by Henry Trump in 1814 and remained in his family until 1850 when it was sold to Richard Choate.[20] The Choate House may have been operated by Israel Owings.

---

[17] Courtesy of Baltimore County Public Library, Randallstown, Maryland.

[18] Inventory of Historic Properties, BA-23. Maryland Historical Trust, Annapolis, Maryland.

[19] Inventory of Historic Properties, BA-16. Maryland Historical Trust, Annapolis, Maryland.

[20] Inventory of Historic Properties, BA-15. Maryland Historical Trust, Annapolis, Maryland.

Sixteen ordinaries were licensed along the Liberty Turnpike, averaging one ordinary every mile and a quarter. No licenses were issued to business concerns and, of the twenty-nine individuals licensed, two were women and twenty-seven were men.

Reisterstown (or Hookstown) Turnpike

Mile Post	Licensee	Year	Approximate Location
2	John Milner	1831	North Avenue
3	Edward Griffin	1830, 1831	Liberty Heights Avenue
4	Louis Larpenter	1830, 1831	Shirley Avenue
4½	John Lewin	1831	Ridgewood Avenue
5	Laban Welch	1830, 1831	Hayward Avenue
5	Joseph Frost	1830, 1831	Hayward Avenue
6½	Andrew McSherry	1830, 1831	Strathmore Avenue
7	Jacob Tayman	1830, 1831	Milford Mill Road
7	Lloyd McAllister	1830, 1831	Milford Mill Road
8	Francis Blackwell	1830, 1831	Slade Avenue
8½	John King	1830, 1831	Sudbrook Lane
9	Philip Waggoner	1831	Woodholme Avenue
10	George Ilgenfritz	1830	Mt. Wilson Lane
10	Joseph Indik	1831	Mt. Wilson Lane
13	Peregrine Gorsuch	1831	Tollgate Road

Mile Post	Licensee	Year	Approximate Location
13	Lemuel Garner	1831	Tollgate Road
13	Jesse Manning	1830	Tollgate Road
13	Michael Great	1831	Tollgate Road
13	John Murphy	1831	Tollgate Road
14	William Dwyer	1831	Delight Road
14	John Morrow	1831	Delight Road
14	William King	1831	Delight Road
14	John Morrow	1831	Delight Road
14	Christian Grove	1831	Delight Road
14	Elizabeth Conn	1831	Delight Road
14	Jacob Hartzell, Jr.	1830, 1831	Delight Road
16	Samuel Harryman	1831	Reisterstown
16	John Thomas	1831	Reisterstown
16	Peter Storm	1831	Reisterstown
16	Margaret McElhert	1831	Reisterstown
16	Solomon Choate	1830, 1831	Reisterstown

Mile Post	Licensee	Year	Approximate Location
16	Jeremiah Ducker	1830, 1831	Reisterstown
16	Nimrod Chapman	1830, 1831	Reisterstown
16	John Fisher	1830	Reisterstown
16	Daniel Ferney	1830, 1831	Reisterstown
16½	George Fisher	1831	Reisterstown
16¾	George Weaver	1831	Reisterstown

The Hookstown Road or Turnpike is one of those names no longer in use and likely unfamiliar to the reader. Named after the village located near its intersection with Garrison Avenue, the Hookstown Road was the name of the Reisterstown Road from the Baltimore City boundary at North Avenue to Reisterstown. Today, the old Hookstown Road or Turnpike is Pennsylvania Avenue from North Avenue to North Fulton Street, then is the Reisterstown Road all of the way to its junction with the Westminster and Hanover Turnpikes in Reisterstown. Gradually, the name Hookstown Road fell into disfavor, probably about the same time that the village was swallowed by the ever-expanding city, replaced by the name Reisterstown Road, the licenses evidently issued during the period of transition. The road was operated as a turnpike, regardless of whether it was called a road or turnpike in the original record.

By far, most of the references to the Hookstown Road in the two lists are for locations between North Avenue and Pikesville, although one license was issued for a trader in Owings Mills, an ordinary in Owings Mills, and an ordinary as far away as Hampstead. Both Jacob

Tayman and Edward Griffin were licensed on the Hookstown Road in 1830, but on the Reisterstown Road in 1831. Numerous licenses were issued at mile posts along the Reisterstown Road, from the vicinity of North Avenue all the way to Reisterstown and beyond. John Stansbury was located on the Hookstown Road; but, the clerk failed to record his mile post, making it impossible to locate the licensee more precisely.

Seven of the original milestones have survived: Mile Stone 5 on the southwest corner of Reisterstown Road and Hayward Avenue; Mile Stone 7 on the northeast corner of Reisterstown Road and Milford Mill Road and Slade Avenue; Mile Stone 9 on the west side of the road, a few hundred feet north of the Beltway; Mile Stone 11 at 9800 Reisterstown Road, on the west side; Mile Stone 14 on the west side at 11418 Reisterstown Road in Delight; and, Mile Stone 15 in front of Franklin High School.[21] Two milestones remain in Reisterstown, Mile Stone 16 opposite 340 Main Street and Mile Stone 17 on the southeast corner of Hanover and Butler Roads.[22] The first tollgate was at Pennsylvania and Fulton Avenues in the city. The second tollgate was located at Woodberry Avenue near Mile Post 3, another near Rogers Avenue, and a third about one thousand feet north of Nicodemus Road.[23]

In 1826, Captain Jeremiah Ducker purchased a half-acre tract in the crook of the intersection between the Hanover and Westminster Turnpikes at a sheriff's sale, now at 1 Hanover Road. He soon built a

---

[21] Hollifield, Page 38.

[22] Inventory of Historic Properties, BA-1333. Maryland Historical Trust, Annapolis, Maryland.

[23] Hollifield, Pages 33-37.

tavern and was licensed in 1830 and 1831.[24] South of Ducker's was Fisher's Tavern on the west side of the turnpike, Forney's Tavern opposite Chatsworth Avenue, Bower's Tavern just north of Cockeys Mill Road, the Yellow Tavern across the turnpike, Reister's Tavern south of Cockeys Mill Road, and Nichols Tavern across the turnpike and just south of Bond Avenue.[25] Either John or George Fisher operated Fisher's Tavern. Daniel Ferney, a hatter by trade, operated Forney's Tavern and Jacob Medairy operated the Yellow Tavern, also later known as Central Hotel, Everhart Tavern, Vondersmith Hotel, and lastly Hobb's Hotel. Daniel Bowers built his tavern with thirty-six rooms before 1800.[26]

In 1829, George Gore sold three lots on the east side of the turnpike on the south side of Bond Avenue to Jacob Decker for $900, who is believed to have operated a tavern at what is now 301-303 Main Street. In 1831, Decker's heirs sold the property to William Frush.[27] Because no one named Decker was licensed in 1830 or 1831, Decker or his heirs may have rented the property to one of the licensees, the tavern apparently later known as the Nichols Tavern.

---

[24] Inventory of Historic Properties, BA-1275. Maryland Historical Trust, Annapolis, Maryland.

[25] McGrain, John W., *Industrial Archaeological Survey of the Northwest Transportation Corridor, Baltimore County, Maryland*, 1975, Page IV-1a. Maryland State Highway Administration, Baltimore, Maryland. (Hereinafter cited as McGrain.)

[26] Goodwin, Louise Bland, *Milestones in the History of Reisterstown, Maryland, 1758-1965.* Unpublished, typewritten manuscript, 1966. Baltimore County Public Library, Reisterstown, Maryland.

[27] Inventory of Historic Properties, BA-894. Maryland Historical Trust, Annapolis, Maryland.

The old Fourteen Mile House was located at Delight and Nicodemus Roads.[28] William Dwyer operated the tavern, situated on the old Lowe tract called *"Food A-Plenty."*[29] In 1833, Jacob Hartzell advertised a meeting to discuss separating Baltimore County from the City to be held at his tavern in Reisterstown.[30] In 1830 and 1831, Jacob Hartzell was licensed at Mile Post 14, about two miles from Reisterstown, possibly indicating a later move to Reisterstown by 1833.

In 1833, David Geiman announced the sale of a tavern stand, then occupied by Michael Great, on the Baltimore Turnpike thirteen miles from the city, near Owings Mills, and consisting of a two-story brick building.[31] Apparently, Michael Great rented the tavern, on the west side of the turnpike near Cedarmere Road, from Geiman in 1830 and 1831, whether he continued to rent after the sale uncertain. Great's Tavern was described as a fine, large place with stables for one hundred horses.[32] The old Gunbarrel Tavern near Gwynnbrook Avenue, now at 11011 Reisterstown Road operated during the early 1800s, by one of the licensees.[33] The proprietor would not allow teamsters and drovers inside, serving them refreshments through a

---

[28] McGrain, Page IV-1a.

[29] Forbes, Marie, *Speaking of Our Past, A Narrative History of Owings Mills, Maryland, 164-1988*, Page 56. Heritage Books, Inc., Westminster, Maryland, 1988. (Hereinafter cited as Forbes.)

[30] Bates, Page 8.

[31] Bates, Page 12.

[32] Forbes, Page 56.

[33] Inventory of Historic Properties, BA-890. Maryland Historical Trust, Annapolis, Maryland.

window. In winter, not wanting to open the window, he would pour the purchased libation out of a small hole through an old gun barrel.[34]

The Wheat Tavern was located where the elementary school is now, but may not have been in operation in 1831.[35] In Owings Mills near the tollgate were the Eight-Square House, Conn's Tavern, and Shull's, whether any of the three were in operation in 1830 and 1831 uncertain.[36] That Elizabeth Conn was licensed nearby suggests that Conn's Tavern may have been closer to Delight than the tollgate. The Twelve Mile House, also known as Fitch's Tavern, was situated next to the railroad on the east side.[37]

At or near the intersection of Craddock Lane were the Tobin House and the Ten Mile House, perhaps operated by George Ilgenfritz or Joseph Indik. Just south of Naylor's Lane, near Mile Post 9, was the Burnt Tavern, possibly operated by Philip Waggoner. The old 8½ Mile House, probably operated by John King, was located near Sudbrook Lane. At or near Mile Post 7 were the Seven Mile House and the Black Horse Tavern (also known as Noblet's), possibly operated by Jacob Tayman or Lloyd McAllister.[38]

The old Wilhelm Tavern, later known as the Breyn-Mawr Hotel was located at the intersection of Glen Avenue, between Mile Post 6 and 7; the Five Mile House was just south of Hayward Avenue, near Belvedere Avenue; the Four Mile House was near Shirley Avenue; the

---

[34] Forbes, Page 56.

[35] Forbes, Page 255.

[36] McGain, Page IV-1a.

[37] Forbes, Page 253.

[38] McGain, Page IV-1a.

Hammett House and Three Mile House were near Liberty Heights Avenue; and, Wooler's Tavern was about midway between North Avenue and Park Circle.[39] At least some of the identified taverns, houses, and hotels probably were operated in 1830 and 1831 by the subject licensees.

A total of twenty-two ordinaries were licensed along the Reisterstown Turnpike between North Avenue and Reisterstown, averaging about one ordinary every three quarters of a mile. All thirty-six licensees were individuals, thirty-four men and two women. The Edward Griffin who was licensed at Mile Post 3 in 1830, most likely is the same man as Edward Griffith who was licensed at the same mile post in 1831. A trader license was issued in 1831 to Laban Welch at Mile Post 5 on Baltimore and Reisters, apparently a misnomer having been licensed at the same mile post on Reisterstown Road the previous year.

---

[39] McGain, Page IV-1a.

Hanover Turnpike

Mile Post	Licensee	Year	Approximate Location
19	William Wooden	1831	Woodensburg
19½	George Baker	1831	Woodensburg
20	Jacob Stick	1830	Fowblesburg
21	Thomas Uppercou	1831	Upperco
22	John Crist	1831	Upperco
22	Joshua Algire	1831	Upperco
23	Andrew Burk	1831	Upperco
24	David Musselman	1831	Carroll County Line
24¾	Henry Null	1831	Trenton Mill Road
26	John Hively	1831	Hampstead
26	Solomon McHanney	1831	Hampstead
27½	Elias Woods	1831	Hampstead
28	Jacob Stick	1831	Hampstead
28	George Bramwell	1831	Hampstead
28	John Murry J	1831	Hampstead

Mile Post	Licensee	Year	Approximate Location
28	Jacob Ebaugh	1831	Hampstead
28	Nicholas Harrison	1831	Hampstead
28	William McIlvaine	1831	Hampstead
28	Henry Lamott	1831	Hampstead
28	William B. Gist	1831	Hampstead
28	William Thompson	1830	Hampstead
30	Baker & Houck	1831	Manchester
30	Dennis Davis	1831	Manchester
30	Joseph Gardner	1831	Manchester
30	George Motter	1830, 1831	Manchester
30	William Crumrine	1831	Manchester
30	Jacob Frick	1831	Manchester
30	Charles Miller	1831	Manchester
30½	George Everhart	1831	Manchester
30½	David Everhart	1832	Manchester
31	Henry Roatbaust	1831	Manchester

Mile Post	Licensee	Year	Approximate Location
32½	George Showers	1831	Melrose
33	Lawrence Freed	1831	Melrose
33	John Wentz	1830, 1831	Melrose
34	John Weaver	1830, 1831	Mason Dixon Line
34	Jacob Houck	1831	Mason Dixon Line

There also seems to have been at least some confusion concerning the Reisterstown and Hanover Turnpikes, possibly because both were operated by the same company and both terminated at Reisterstown. In 1830, John Wentz of Manchester was licensed on the Reisterstown Turnpike; but, in 1831 he was licensed on the Hanover Turnpike at the same mile post. The Hanover Turnpike, then officially part of the Baltimore and Reisterstown Turnpike Road Company and now Maryland Route 30, began in Reisterstown, at the junction of the Reisterstown and Westminster Turnpikes; proceeded in a northerly direction, through Woodensburg, Fowblesburg, Hampstead, and Manchester; and, ended at the Mason Dixon Line near Mile Post 34.

Tollgates were located at Woodensburg, Fowblesburg, and another probably at the state line. One gate keeper's house, built circa 1811, still stands at 15405 Hanover Pike, just north of the Old Hanover Road.[40] Three mile stones remain, Mile Stone 17 at Butler Road,

---

[40] Inventory of Historic Properties, BA-1166. Maryland Historical Trust, Annapolis, Maryland.

Mile Stone 18 at 13233 Old Hanover Road, and Mile Stone 23 about five hundred feet north of Dover Road.[41]

Nathan Chapman was licensed at Mile Post 17½ near Reisterstown, perhaps in the vicinity of Emory Grove and the Reisterstown railroad station. William T. Heston was licensed at Mile Post 19 near Reisterstown, possibly in the vicinity of Woodensburg, but whether east or west of the small village uncertain. Andrew Burk was licensed both as a trader and an ordinary. In 1830, Jacob Stick was licensed at Mile Post 20; but, in 1831, he was licensed at Mile Post 28, either the clerk erring in recording the mile post or Jacob Stick moving his business from Fowblesburg to Hampstead, the latter possibly more likely. In 1830, John Wentz was licensed at Mile Post 33; but, in 1831, he was licensed at Mile Post 33½, whether the discrepancy indicates he had moved his business or simply was more accurate in describing its location uncertain, again the latter possibly more likely.

Immediately to the north of the Mason Dixon Line, Sherman's Tavern was situated on the turnpike at Sherman's Church Road, near St. David's (Sherman's) Lutheran Church.[42] Four miles to the south sat an unnamed tavern near Bachman Valley Road, Shower's Tavern at Manchester, and still others clustered at Hampstead, including Lamott's.

The oldest house in Manchester, in 1882 owned by Edward Oursler, was formerly kept as a tavern by Christian Heibly. On the lot owned by Mr. Brinkman, the jeweler, in 1882, a tavern once stood.[43]

---

[41] Hollifield, Page 38.

[42] McGain, Page IV-37.

[43] Scharf, Page 884.

The legislation creating Carroll County in 1837 described the boundaries of the new Manchester District, including *"...thence to Michael Baker's Tavern on the Hanover and Baltimore turnpike road...,"* placing Baker's tavern between Manchester and Hampstead.[44]

Colonel Johns sold a log warehouse to John Cox, the first actual settler in Hampstead, who converted the building into a tavern which he kept for many years, subsequently selling it to Henry Lamott.[45] Henry Lamott kept the tavern forty-five years, dying in 1851. John Fowble kept the first store in town and Peter Frank kept the first tavern, succeeded by John Cox.

In 1833, Jacob Ebaugh announced the sale of property to be held at the tavern of Benjamin Davis in Hampstead, 26 miles from Baltimore on the turnpike road, the property consisting of the tavern stand and 3¼ acres of land then occupied by Davis with barn and sheds.[46] Jacob Ebaugh apparently operated the tavern on his property in 1831, but rented his tavern to Benjamin Davis by 1833. Later that same year, George Belt, on an order from a Baltimore County court and acting as trustee, offered for sale several parcels of real estate, including a tavern stand and store in Hampstead.[47]

In 1837, Samuel Moale, Jr. sold the Spring Garden Hotel property to John Stansbury. One of the most prominent commercial buildings in

---

[44] Scharf, Page 883.

[45] Scharf, Page 891.

[46] Bates, Marlene and Martha Reamy, *Abstracts of Carroll County Newspapers, 1831-1846*, Page 5. Family Line Publicaions, Wesminster, Maryland, 1988. (Hereinafter cited as Bates.)

[47] Bates, Page 8.

Hampstead, the old hotel was torn down in the 1970s, purportedly containing a log section of the first building in the town.[48] The old hotel probably was operated by one of the licensees in Hampstead.

Sapp's Tavern, as it was last known, was torn down in the 1950s to make way for an automobile dealer's showroom. Richard Richards gave the original lease for the property, now located on the east side of Main Street on the south side of Shiloh Avenue, to Jacob Ebaugh in 1809.[49] It seems unlikely, but not impossible, that the same Jacob Ebaugh operated the tavern in 1831.

John Crist owned and operated the Blue Ball Tavern until his death in 1839.[50] His tavern, barn, and other improvements sat on a tract of 39 acres, 1 rood, and 12 perches, being parts of tracts named *Ropewalk*, *Baxter's Folly*, and *Gittinger's Farm*, located near Mile Post 22, in sight of the old German church. Roods and perches are old units of land measurement, one rood equaling one quarter acre and forty perches equaling one rood, making the old Blue Ball Tavern tract 39.325 acres in size. The old German church today is St. Paul's (Algire's) Lutheran Church on the northeast corner of the turnpike and Dover Road, placing the Blue Ball Tavern no farther than a few hundred feet to the south of the church, possibly in the vicinity of Carrollton Road.

---

[48] Inventory of Historic Properties, CR-1269. Maryland Historical Trust, Annapolis, Maryland.

[49] Inventory of Historic Properties, CR-1264. Maryland Historical Trust, Annapolis, Maryland.

[50] Baltimore County Chancery Court Records, Chancery Papers, MSA No. S512, *Elizabeth Crist, et al vs. John Crist, et al*, 1840, File No., 17,898-6798-1/4, 1-37-3-73. Maryland State Archives, Annapolis, Maryland.

Twenty-seven ordinaries were licensed on the Hanover Turnpike between Reisterstown and the Mason Dixon Line, averaging about one ordinary every two thirds of a mile. The Old Hanover Road, bypassed with the construction of the turnpike, leaves the present-day Hanover Road at Woodensburg and merges back at Fowblesburg. George Baker may have resided on the Old Hanover Road. A license was issued to a business concern, Baker & Houck, near Manchester, and thirty-four licenses were issued to individuals, all of them men.

Westminster Turnpike

Mile Post	Licensee	Year	Approximate Location
20	William Corbin	1831	Finksburg
20	William Young	1831	Finksburg
20	William Horner	1831	Finksburg
20	Mordicai G. Cockey	1831	Finksburg
20	Thomas Ward	1831	Finksburg
22	Samuel Cable	1831	Reese Road
22	Lemuel Garner	1831	Reese Road
22	Jesse Manning	1831	Reese Road
23	John Robertson	1831	Tara Oaks Court
23	William Jameson	1830, 1831	Tara Oaks Court
24	Abraham Kuntz	1830	New Washington Road
24	Jacob Taney	1832	New Washington Road
24	Edmund Garner	1831	New Washington Road
24½	George Batson	1831	Westminster
25	David Hartzell	1831	Westminster

Mile Post	Licensee	Year	Approximate Location
25	Honour Woolry	1831	Westminster
25½	Peter Earbaugh	1831	Westminster

The Westminster Turnpike, constructed largely with convict labor, began in Reisterstown at the intersection of the Reisterstown and Hanover Turnpikes, proceeded in a northwesterly direction through Finksburg, and ended in Westminster about Mile Post 25. The clerk first noted that he did not issue the license to Abraham Kuntz, then apparently crossed through the notation, indicating that Abraham Kuntz was licensed. Mile Stone 19 is located on the old turnpike road about midway between Glen Falls Road and the edge of Liberty Reservoir.[51] Like its sister Hanover Turnpike, the Westminster Turnpike officially was a branch of the Reisterstown Turnpike.

Joseph Stansbury was licensed at Mile Post 26 near the turnpike, probably located near Westminster. John Coleman was licensed as a trader at Mile Post 27, past Westminster. Six trader licenses were issued along the turnpike to Mordecai G. Cockey, Thomas Ward, Lemuel Garner, Jesse Manning, William Jameson, Edmund Garner, and John Coleman. Eleven ordinary licenses were issued, only one to a woman, averaging one ordinary about every half mile.

The author recalls being told in his youth about the Eighteen Mile House, near the intersection of Glen Falls Road, perhaps at 1100 Westminster Road, for many years the site of a restaurant or tavern. The town of Finksburg was laid out in 1813 by a Mr. Quigly, a

---

[51] Hollifield, Page 38.

contractor on the turnpike, then under construction. Adam Fink built the first house and kept a tavern there, succeeded by William Horner, Sr., who kept the inn for twenty years.[52] William Horner was licensed in 1831.

In 1834, the trustees announced a public sale of certain lands to be held at Batson's Tavern near Mile Stone 24 on the Westminster Turnpike.[53] George Batson was licensed in 1831.

---

[52] Scharf, Page 868.

[53] Bates, Page 13.

Deer Park Road

Mile Post	Licensee	Year	Approximate Location
16	Thomas Porter	1831	Berryman's Lane
16	Archibald Porter	1831	Berryman's Lane
16	William Garey	1830, 1831	Berryman's Lane
25	Martico M. Welch	1830, 1831	Sykesville Road
25	Nicholas Buckingham	1831	Sykesville Road
25	Benjamin Kelly	1830	Sykesville Road

Deer Park Road begins at Harrisonville on the Liberty Road near Mile Post 12½, heading north through Soldiers Delight, turning west at Berryman's Lane near Mile Post 16, crossing the Patapsco River, heading in a northwesterly direction to its end at the Sykesville Road, near Mile Post 25, about four miles south of Westminster. Deer Park Road was not operated as a turnpike. An ordinary license was issued to Benjamin Kelley at Mile Post 25 in 1830 and at Mile Post 26 in 1831. Because Mile Post 26 is beyond the end of Deer Park Road, the Kelly ordinary probably was located near the intersection of Deer Park Road and the Sykesville Road. Five trader licenses, to Thomas Porter, Archibald Porter, William Garey, Martico M. Welch, and Nicholas Buckingham, and one ordinary license were issued, the twelve-mile stretch of road between the Liberty Turnpike and the Sykesville Road making for a rather dry journey compared to most of the other roads and turnpikes.

Falls Road Turnpike

Mile Post	Licensee	Year	Approximate Location
1¼	Alexander Maydwell	1831	North Avenue
1¼	James Gibbs	1831	North Avenue
1¾	Zacheas Durham	1832	Hampden
1¾	William Moon	1830	Hampden
2	Catherine Yeager	1831	Hampden Heights
4	John R. Gwynn	1831	Cold Spring Lane
4	John Macklan	1831	Cold Spring Lane
5½	Adam Mungan	1830, 1831	Mt. Washington
5½	Robert S. Hollins	1831	Mt. Washington
6	David Peden & Co.	1831	Lake Avenue
6	Dennis Morrison	1831	Lake Avenue
7	Levi Gibbs	1830	Pimlico Road
8	Andrew Hall	1831	Old Court Road
9	Robert Ambrose	1830	Joppa Road
9	Darius Litzinger	1831	Joppa Road

Mile Post	Licensee	Year	Approximate Location
9½	Lewis Bowen	1831	Seminary Avenue
11	Samuel Cockey	1831	Padonia Road
13	John Burnham	1830, 1831	Ridge Road
13	Ephraim Tipton	1830	Ridge Road
14	Levi Merryman	1831	Shawan
15	John Leaf	1831	Gentsville
15	Samuel McCoy	1831	Gentsville
16	Ely Scott	1831	Geist Meeting House
18	Amelia B. Gill	1831	Butler
18	Kinsey Johns	1830, 1831	Butler
18	George Mallonee	1831	Butler
20	Benjamin Simpers	1832	Benson Mill Road
23	John Zouck	1831	Brick Store Road
24	David Hoover	1830	Grave Run Mills
26	John Lamott	1832	Mason Dixon Line

Chartered in 1805, the Falls Turnpike Road Company was directed to construct a road beginning at the ford near Patterson and Strickler's Mill, then north as near the Falls as practicable for a good road, over the Bare Hills, west of Benjamin Bowen's house, west on or near Job Hunt's land, to the crossroads near Richard Caton's limekiln, near Green Spring Valley Road in Brooklandville. The Falls Road north of Brooklandville was a free road and never operated as a turnpike. A local guidebook in 1832 noted the turnpike, *"passes over a most romantic and beautiful route, and makes one of the pleasantest rides in the neighborhood of the city."*

The original Falls Road Turnpike approximately followed the Jones Falls from the Baltimore City boundary at North Avenue, generally in a northerly direction, to Brooklandville. The Falls Road then continued in a northerly direction to the Mason Dixon Line at Grave Run Mills. John Leaf was licensed as an ordinary promptly at the start of each license year in 1830 and 1831 at Mile Post 15 near Gentsville. John Leef, no doubt the same man, was licensed as a trader at the same location effective September 29, 1831. Four other men, John Burnham, John Macklan, Darius Litzinger, and Zacheas Durham, were licensed both as traders and ordinaries. The first tollgate was located just north of North Avenue, a second just north of Cold Spring Lane, and the third tollgate near Old Court Road. Mile Stone 7 is just north of Coppermine Terrace and Mile Stone 8 is on the northeast corner of Falls Road and Old Court Road.[54]

Eighteen ordinaries were licensed along the Falls Road Turnpike, averaging one ordinary every one and four tenths miles. One license was issued to a business concern, David Peden & Co. Of the twenty-eight licenses issued to individuals, two were issued to women and twenty-six were issued to men.

---

[54] Hollifield, Page 43.

John R. Gwynn built the Brooklandville House as a tavern on the west side of the turnpike near Mile Post 8, now known as the Valley Inn at 10501 Falls Road.[55] In 1831, John R. Gwynn was licensed at Mile Post 4, near Cold Spring Lane, evidently later moving to Brooklandville.

---

[55] Inventory of Historic Properties, BA-218. Maryland Historical Trust, Annapolis, Maryland.

York Turnpike

Mile Post	Licensee	Year	Approximate Location
1	Richard Hamilton	1831	31st Street
1	Elizabeth Dendy	1831	31st Street
1½	Henry Starr	1830, 1831	Bretton Place
2	William W. Riggen	1830	43rd Street
2	Martin Bowers	1830	43rd Street
2	David Kennedy	1830	43rd Street
2	William Bacon	1831	43rd Street
2	William Phipps	1831	43rd Street
2	Ann Margaret Bowers	1831	43rd Street
2½	John Maxwell	1830, 1831	Cold Spring Lane
3	Peter Blatchley	1830, 1831	Homeland Avenue
3	Thomas Wilson	1831	Homeland Avenue
3	Micajah Tracey	1831	Homeland Avenue
3½	William L. Moran	1831	Hollen Road
4	Joseph Allison	1830, 1831	Hollen Road

Mile Post	Licensee	Year	Approximate Location
4	Linnard Zeney	1830	Hollen Road
4	Maria Eichelberger	1831	Hollen Road
4	John Crouse	1831	Hollen Road
5	Elizabeth Mumma	1831	Hatherleigh Road
7	Thomas Wallace	1830	Allegheny Avenue
7	James Perigo	1830, 1831	Allegheny Avenue
7	George Shealey	1831	Allegheny Avenue
7	Nathaniel Ware	1831	Allegheny Avenue
7	David Freeland	1831	Allegheny Avenue
8½	Samuel Walker	1830, 1831	Bellona Avenue
10½	Nicholas Cornelius	1831	Rose Street
12	John Clarke	1831	Water Bird Court
12	Jacob Worley	1830, 1831	Water Bird Court
12	James Merford	1832	Water Bird Court
13	William Badders	1831	Blenheim Road
13½	Adam Smyzer	1831	Wight Avenue

Mile Post	Licensee	Year	Approximate Location
14	Elizabeth Brookhart	1830, 1831	Shawan Road
14	Nehemiah Price	1831	Shawan Road
14	E. G. Kilbourne	1831	Shawan Road
16	Samuel Webb	1831	Loveton Circle
16	Alexis Green	1830, 1831	Loveton Circle
16	Thomas King	1831	Loveton Circle
17	Samuel Stubbins	1830, 1831	Sparks Road
17	Caleb Hunt	1831	Sparks Road
17	Mahlon C. Price	1830, 1831	Sparks Road
17	William Westerman	1831	Sparks Road
19	Joshua Gorsuch	1830, 1831	Upper Glencoe Road
20	William Slade	1830, 1831	Piney Hill Road
20	Daniel Conn	1831	Piney Hill Road
21	James Marsh	1831	Monkton Road
21	William Tipton	1830, 1831	Monkton Road
21	Janett Tipton	1831	Monkton Road

Mile Post	Licensee	Year	Approximate Location
21	John Rutledge	1831	Monkton Road
21	William Roe	1830, 1831	Monkton Road
21	Dixon Morton	1831	Troyer Road
22	Joseph Bryan	1830, 1831	Bunker Hill Road
22	James Wilson	1831	Bunker Hill Road
23	Ephraim Cox	1832	Woodhall Vineyards
24	Benjamin Garrett	1830, 1831	Middletown Road
24	Peter Smyser	1830, 1831	Middletown Road
24	William Ewing	1831	Middletown Road
24	George Beckley	1830, 1831	Middletown Road
24	Joshua Spindler	1831	Middletown Road
24	Peter Ewing	1831	Middletown Road
25	John Jones	1831	Calder Road
27	Joshua Standiford	1831	Kauffman Road
27	Frederick Kauffman	1831	Kauffman Road
27	George Bond	1831	Kauffman Road

Mile Post	Licensee	Year	Approximate Location
28	Teego Cooper	1831	Jordan Saw Mill Road
30	Thomas Craig	1830	Maryland Line
30	William Hunter	1831	Maryland Line
30	Samuel Ulrich	1831	Maryland Line
30	Charles Small	1831	Maryland Line
30	Isaac Marshall	1831	Maryland Line
30	Jesse Marshall	1831	Maryland Line
30	John Michael	1831	Maryland Line
30	Andrew Turner	1831	Maryland Line
30	Aquila Sparks	1830	Maryland Line

From the Colonial period, the first road from Baltimore to York crossed the Gunpowder River at Meredith's Ford, now submerged under Loch Raven Reservoir near Dulaney Valley Road about Mile Post 12, and generally followed Jarrettsville Road northward to the vicinity of Merryman's Mill Road. The next portion of the old road long has been abandoned. From Paper Mill Road, Old York Road headed northward past St. James Church about Mile Post 19, crossed into Harford County about Mile Post 21, crossed back into Baltimore County, near Shane and Mile Post 26, and headed northwesterly to the town of Maryland Line. In 1773, George Washington traveled from

York to Baltimore, stopping at Slade's Tavern near Manor Road. Almony's Tavern was located where Troyer Road intersects Old York Road. There were two Sutton's Taverns, one just south of the Little Gunpowder Falls crossing and one near Graystone Road in Shane. The Blackhorse Tavern was situated in Harford County at the crossroads that still bears that name.[56]

Thirteen of the licensees were described as on Old York Road: William Badders at Mile Post 13; Samuel Webb, Thomas King, and Alexis Green at Mile Post 16; Dixon Morton at Mile Post 21; Peter Ewing, William Ewing, and George Beckley at Mile Post 24; Teego Cooper at Mile Post 28; Isaac Marshall, Jesse Marshall, John Zimmerman, and John Michael at Mile Post 30; and, Peter Hoffman at Mile Post 34.

At Mile Post 13, William Badders may have been near the present intersection of Jarrettsville Pike and Blenheim Road, rather than the old turnpike and Sherwood Road. Mile Post 16 probably was near the intersection of Old York Road and Paper Mill Road, which licensees located there or along the turnpike near Loveton Circle uncertain. Dixon Morton may have operated Almony's Tavern near Mile Post 21. Because Mile Post 24 appears to have been in Harford County, the three persons licensed there probably were on the turnpike and not on the Old York Road. Teego Cooper was licensed at Mile Post 28, possibly near the intersection of Old York Road and Jordan Saw Mill Road, rather than near the turnpike and Downes Road. Mile Post 30 was at Maryland Line, on the turnpike, not the Old York Road.

---

[56] Clemens, Shirley B., and Clarence E. Clemens, *From Marble Hill to Maryland Line, An Informal History of Northern Baltimore County.* Privately printed, 1976. (Hereinafter cited as Clemens.)

The York Turnpike commenced at North Avenue on the northwest corner of Greenmount Cemetery, headed northward along present-day Greenmount Avenue to the vicinity of 43rd Street, then continued northward generally along present-day York Road to Towson at Mile Post 7, through Cockeysville, Hereford, and Parkton, ending at the town of Maryland Line on the south side of the Pennsylvania border about one half mile past Mile Post 30. The southernmost portion of the turnpike followed the high ground called *Britain's Ridge* dividing the Jones Falls and Herring Run watersheds.

Another Old York Road, apparently created by the construction of the turnpike, generally parallels Greenmount Avenue and York Road from Vineyard Lane northward to Radnor Avenue, the remainder of the original alignment long ago obliterated by more modern development.

During the 1830s, a turnpike company office and tollgate were located immediately south of the Pennsylvania border near Mile Post 30, a second tollgate and company office at Wiseburg, a third tollgate at Piney Hill north of Cold Bottom Road and Mile Post 19, a fourth at the foot of Fifteen Mile Hill, a fifth at Towson, and a sixth in Waverly.[57] The Waverly tollgate was located at Vineyard Lane.[58] Built circa 1790, the toll keeper's house at the fourth tollgate was adjacent to the turnpike on the west side, at Mile Post 15, just north of the Thornton Mill Road intersection, the modern address 13822 York Road.[59]

---

[57] Hollifield, Pages 51-57.

[58] *Village Life Goes On Along Old York Road.* Self-guided Walking Tour of Waverly, Better Waverly Community Organization, August 2010. (Hereinafter cited as Waverly.)

[59] Inventory of Historic Properties, BA-190. Maryland Historical Trust, Annapolis, Maryland.

A total of nine mile stones have survived:

- Mile Stone 9, north of Margate Road in Lutherville
- Mile Stone 10, north of Northwood Drive in Timonium
- Mile Stone 16, half mile north of Phoenix Road
- Mile Stone 19, at the Gorsuch Tavern, north of Upper Glencoe Road
- Mile Stone 20, fifteen hundred feet north of Piney Hill Road
- Mile Stone 21, Monkton Road in Hereford
- Mile Stone 25, Calder Road in Parkton
- Mile Stone 29, south of Old York Road
- Mile Stone 30, 21,419 York Road in Maryland Line.

Both Elizabeth Dendy and Richard Hamilton were licensed at Mile Post 1, placing them near the corner of Hoffman Street, inside the city limits. Because neither person is listed in the 1829 city directory, both probably were on the county side of North Avenue. Most likely, it was Nehemiah Price who was licensed at Mile Post 14, rather than Price Nehemiah.

Thomas Wallace, James Perigo, Nicholas Cornelius, Samuel Webb, Nathaniel Ware, Joshua Standiford, John Clarke, and Henry Wier were licensed both as ordinaries and traders. James Perigo was licensed at Mile Post 7 in 1830 and at Mile Post 8 in 1831; but, whether he had businesses at two locations or simply changed the description of the location from year to year uncertain. Jonathan Plowman and Henry Wier were licensed at Mile Post 26 near the turnpike, possibly at or near the village of Bentley Springs. John Zimmerman was licensed at Mile Post 30 near the turnpike, possibly on Harris Mill Road. Levi Merryman was licensed at Mile Post 14 near the turnpike, possibly at Phoenix Station. William Brooks was licensed at Mile Post 18 near the turnpike, possibly on Upper Glencoe Road. Edward Orrick was licensed at Mile Post 20 near the turnpike, perhaps located in the vicinity of White Hall. Peter Hoffman was licensed at Mile Post 34, a location about four miles into Pennsylvania.

The old Cold Spring Hotel was situated in Govanstown, probably near Cold Spring Lane at Mile Post 2½.[60] The old Eight Mile House, long since demolished, stood at 1310 York Road about one thousand feet south of Seminary Avenue, possibly operated by Samuel Walker in 1830 and 1831.[61]

The old Cockeysville Hotel, near Mile Post 12, was built circa 1810 by Joshua F. Cockey, who apparently lived in the hotel. After the builder's death, the disposition of his estate was decided by the Chancery Court, the tavern going to his son Joshua Frederick Cockey. The plat of subdivision dated 1832 shows a drawing of a house with chimneys at either end labeled "Joshua F. Cockey's Tavern." [62] During the litigation over the estate, the tavern apparently was operated by someone else.

Dickenson Gorsuch built the old Gorsuch Tavern in 1813, located on the east side of the turnpike near Mile Stone 19, just north of the Upper Glencoe Road intersection, at

---

[60] Waverly.

[61] Inventory of Historic Properties, BA-1755. Maryland Historical Trust, Annapolis, Maryland.

[62] Inventory of Historic Properties, BA-515. Maryland Historical Trust, Annapolis, Maryland.

the modern address of 15911 York Road. Captain Joshua Gorsuch, owner of the ship *Bon Advenure*, seafarer, and world traveler, purchased the 27-acre parcel in 1817 and operated the tavern until his death in 1844.[63]

Andrew Hacks purchased the old Milton Inn, now at 14833 York Road in Sparks, at a sheriff's sale in 1829 for $1,450, the property then described as *"...two acres and twenty-four square perches of land situate on the York Road about seventeen miles from Baltimore. The improvements consist of a large stone tavern, stables, and a blacksmith shop; also a quantity of household and kitchen furniture."*[64] Caleb Hunt purchased the tavern in 1848, probably after leasing the property and operating the tavern for a number of years.

There was an old log house at the corner of Bunker Hill Road, operated as a tavern as early as circa 1810, still standing in 1925, but in ruins, perhaps operated by Joseph Bryan or James Wilson in 1830.[65]

The Halfway House, also known as the Wiseburg Inn or Tavern, constructed by John Wise in 1810, is located on the west side of York Road at Wiseburg Road, between Mile Posts 23 and 24. Peter Smyser purchased the property from John Wise prior to 1830. The Halfway House was larger than most other taverns or inns on the turnpike north of Baltimore.[66] Pleasant Hunter purchased the

---

[63] Inventory of Historic Properties, BA-130. Maryland Historical Trust, Annapolis, Maryland.

[64] Inventory of Historic Properties, BA-64. Maryland Historical Trust, Annapolis, Maryland.

[65] Clemens.

[66] Inventory of Historic Properties, BA-62. Maryland Historical Trust, Annapolis, Maryland.

property circa 1840, operating the old inn for many years. Adjacent to the Halfway House was a building, owned by the turnpike company and used as a residence and offices, long since demolished, and a toll gate.

Mile Stone 30 is situated about midway between Old York Road and Old Harris Mill Road in the town of Maryland Line at 21419 York Road, slightly more than one half mile south of the Mason Dixon Line, on the property of the historic Jones House.[67] The Maryland Line Hotel probably was built by John Walker on land inherited by Jesse Lowe in 1824. Doctor Ephraim Bell purchased the property on the west side of the turnpike in 1833. The old hotel, if it was in existence in 1831, now is located at 21520 York Road.[68]

Only John Clarke, Joshua Standiford, Henry Wier, and Nathaniel Ware were licensed both as ordinaries and traders. Twenty-one ordinaries were licensed, about one ordinary every one and four tenths miles. Of the seventy-two licensees, only seven were women, the remaining sixty-five men.

---

[67] Inventory of Historic Properties, BA-1986. Maryland Historical Trust, Annapolis, Maryland.

[68] Inventory of Historic Properties, BA-992. Maryland Historical Trust, Annapolis, Maryland.

Harford Turnpike

Mile Post	Licensee	Year	Approximate Location
1¼	James Cullimore	1831	20th Street
1½	Joseph Sewell	1830	Darley Avenue
1½	William W. Riggin	1831	Darley Avenue
1½	Thomas Lewis	1831	Darley Avenue
1¾	William Hague	1830	Friends Cemetery
2½	Catherine America	1830	Erdman Avenue
2½	George Gelbach	1830	Erdman Avenue
2½	John Lemley	1831	Erdman Avenue
2½	John Ertman	1831	Erdman Avenue
3	James Jones	1831	Curran Drive
3	James Willingham	1830	Curran Drive
3¾	Caleb Bishop	1830	Markley Avenue
3¾	Grace Mitchell	1831	Markley Avenue
4	Ann Moran	1831	Rosekemp Avenue
5½	Joshua H. Kidd	1831	Fleetwood Avenue

Mile Post	Licensee	Year	Approximate Location
5½	James Wheeler	1831	Fleetwood Avenue
6	John Harker	1831	Rosalie Avenue
6½	William Gray	1830	Taylor Avenue
7	Elijah Burton	1830	Texas Avenue
8	John Henshaw	1830	2nd Avenue
8	Charles Canoles	1831	2nd Avenue
9	Moses Parlett	1831	Summit Avenue
9	George Bishop	1831	Summit Avenue
9	Susan Pernie	1831	Summit Avenue
10	Acsah Buck	1830	South of Gunpowder Falls
11	Thomas Parlett	1831	North of Gunpowder Falls
12	James Burton	1830	Long Green Pike
14	James McClure	1831	Hutschenreuer Road
15	Charles Baker	1831	Vista View Court
15	Walter Martin	1830	Vista View Court
16	Garnett Watkins	1830	New Cut Road

Mile Post	Licensee	Year	Approximate Location
16	Samuel Watkins	1831	New Cut Road

The Baltimore and Harford Turnpike Company, chartered in 1816, began construction almost immediately. The original Harford Turnpike in Baltimore County generally followed the modern Harford Avenue, from North Avenue, about Mile Post 1, then the northern city boundary, proceeded generally in a northeasterly direction, through Parkville, and ended at the Little Gunpowder Falls, the Harford County boundary, about Mile Post 17, just south of the village of Reckordville.

The first tollgate was opposite Hillen Road, the gate keeper's house on the southeast side, next to the entrance to Clifton Park. The second tollgate, near Hiss Avenue in Lavender Hill, now Parkville, was not constructed until 1850. The third tollgate was erected just south of the Gunpowder Falls in 1819. In 1827, Jacob A. Grace was appointed gate keeper at the third gate, doing such a fine job he was commended by the company for *"his particular attention in collecting the tolls"* in 1831, 1832, 1833, and 1834, awarded a $25 bonus each year and a raise in salary to $150 per year in 1834.[69] The fourth tollgate located just north of Dampman's Tavern at Fork was not constructed until 1860. Just north of the Big Gunpowder Falls, the Northern Branch of the Harford Turnpike went along present-day Factory Road and Long Green Pike to the Little Gunpowder Falls.

Only three milestones survive on the old turnpike: Mile Stone 11 at 10910 Harford Road about one half mile north of Gunpowder Falls, Mile Stone 12 just north of the junction with Long Green Pike, and Mile Stone 13 just south of Hartley Mill Road.[70]

Old Harford Road begins at the intersection of Glenmore Avenue in Hamilton, about Mile Post 5½, proceeds in a more northerly direction, winding its way more or less parallel to the old turnpike, terminating at the Maryland Training School for Boys.

Wright's Hotel, located on the turnpike just south of Fork Meeting House, across from the Regwood Road intersection, was a popular stop with travelers. It was here that Major Harry Gilmor, on his famous raid through Baltimore County in 1864, sent his Ordnance Sergeant Fields, who had been mortally wounded by Ishmael Day.[71]

Dampman's Hotel, on the northeast corner of Harford Road and Sunshine Avenue, was used primarily by farmers traveling along the

---

[69] *Baltimore and Harford Turnpike*. Copies of pages 71 through 77 of a larger, unknown document. Special Collections Department, University of Baltimore Library, Baltimore, Maryland.

[70] Hollifield, Page 74.

[71] Inventory of Historic Properties, BA-247. Maryland Historical Trust, Annapolis, Maryland.

old turnpike. Known to have been built before 1865, it is uncertain whether the property was the site of a tavern in 1831.[72]

Samuel Watkins and Thomas Parlett were licensed both as ordinaries and traders. In 1830, Aquila Sparks was licensed as a trader at Mile Post 30 on old Harford Road and as an ordinary at Mile Post 30 on old York Road. Because, Mile Post 30 on the Harford Turnpike would have been well into Harford County, his ordinary and trading business probably were located at Maryland Line on the York Turnpike. Thirty ordinaries were licensed along the turnpike, averaging two ordinaries per mile. Of the thirty-two licensees, five were women and twenty-eight were men.

---

[72] Inventory of Historic Properties, BA-249. Maryland Historical Trust, Annapolis, Maryland.

Bel Air Turnpike

Mile Post	Licensee	Year	Approximate Location
2	Elisha Battee	1830, 1831	North Avenue
2	Catherine Neukirk	1831	North Avenue
2½	Samuel B. Hugo	1831	Lawnview Avenue
2½	John G. Linsley	1831	Lawnview Avenue
2¾	Garrett Franklin	1831	Mayfield Avenue
3	John Strickert	1830	Herring Run Park
3	Richard Bowers	1831	Herring Run Park
6	George Fuller	1831	Northern Parkway
9	Patrick Mooney	1831	Necker Avenue
10	Catherine Bishop	1831	Joppa Road
14	Abraham King	1831	Buck Hill Road
14	Ishmael Day	1831	Buck Hill Road
16	Michael McBlair	1830	New Cut Road

The Bel Air and Jerusalem Turnpike Company was not authorized until 1859 to construct and operate a turnpike following the Bel Air Road to Kingsville, then Jerusalem Road to the county line.

Apparently, the road was operated as a turnpike before that time, possibly by the county. In 1831, the Bel Air Turnpike started at the Baltimore City boundary on North Avenue adjacent to the northwestern corner of Baltimore Cemetery and continued generally in a northeasterly direction to the Little Gunpowder Falls, the Harford County boundary, at Jerusalem Mills. The first tollgate was located at Sinclair Lane and another at Joppa Road was not erected until much later. Two milestones have survived, Mile Stone 12, at 11501 Bel Air Road, and Mile Stone 14, on the south side of Jerusalem Road just north of Buck Hill Road.[73]

Elisha Battee and Michael McBlair were licensed both as traders and ordinaries. Ishmael Day was licensed as a trader at Mile Post 14 near

the Bel Air Turnpike, possibly in the vicinity of the old Perry Hall estate. The Ishmael Day house is situated on the north side of Sunshine Avenue, about one mile east of Fork, roughly midway between the Harford and Bel Air Turnpikes.[74] The house, burned

---

[73] Hollifield, Page 79.

[74] Inventory of Historic Properties, BA-133. Maryland Historical Trust, Annapolis, Maryland.

by Confederates in 1864 and later repaired, may not be where he lived in 1831, although the location midway between the turnpikes is suggestive. Eleven ordinaries were licensed along Bel Air Turnpike, averaging one ordinary every one and a half miles. In all, twelve licenses were issued to individuals, ten of them to men and two to women.

Philadelphia Turnpike

Mile Post	Licensee	Year	Approximate Location
2	Elizabeth Stapleton	1830, 1831	East Avenue
2	Frederick Brandt	1830	East Avenue
2	Francis Herman Kaase	1831	East Avenue
2½	Mary Brockam	1831	Haven Street
2½	John Murry	1831	Haven Street
4	William Allen	1830	North Point Road
4	Leonard Keplinger	1831	North Point Road
5	Thomas Arnold	1830	Rosedale Heights Avenue
6	Robert McCauley	1830, 1831	Seling Avenue
10	John Burk of Benj.	1830, 1831	Nottingwood Road
12	Thomas Christopher	1831	Ebenezer Road
12	George Hawkins	1830, 1831	Ebenezer Road
12½	Charles Carnan	1831	Joppa Road
13½	Jonathan Vanhorn	1830, 1831	Lloyd Avenue
15	Benjamin Burk & Son	1830, 1831	Raphael Road

Mile Post	Licensee	Year	Approximate Location
15½	John W. Onion	1830, 1831	Pfeffers Road

Established in 1814, the Baltimore and Havre de Grace Turnpike was known at various times as the Post Road, Old Post Road, and Philadelphia Road or Turnpike. In 1831, the Philadelphia Turnpike generally followed Pulaski Highway within the city and the Philadelphia Road in the county, starting near Loneys Lane about Mile Post 2, continuing in a northeasterly direction, and ending at Little Gunpowder Falls, the Harford County boundary at Mile Post 16. The first tollgate was at Orangeville, just east of the Hebrew Friendship Cemetery. The second toll gate was at Mile Stone 10, near Nottingwood Road. The third tollgate was located at the Little Gunpowder Falls crossing. Only Mile Stone 8 has survived, at 8919 Philadelphia Road.[75]

In 1831, East Avenue was the approximate eastern city boundary. John W. Onion was licensed a Mile Post 15½ in 1830 and at Mile Post 16 in 1831, probably indicating the imprecise nature of the location descriptions rather than his moving his ordinary such a short distance. In 1877, a man named J. W. Onion resided approximately one mile due west of the tollgate on the Philadelphia Turnpike. Elisha Coe was licensed at Mile Post 8½ near the Philadelphia Road, possibly at or near Rossville. Jacob H. Minnickhyson was licensed at Mile Post 16 near the Philadelphia Road, possibly in the vicinity of the old Upper Falls Post Office.

---

[75] Hollifield, Page 82.

Mary Brookens was licensed as an ordinary at Mile Post 2½ in 1830. The following year, Mary Brockam was licensed as an ordinary and Mary Brochans was licensed as a trader, both at Mile Post 2½. The three licensees very likely are the same woman, the correct spelling not apparent only from the license records.

Thirteen ordinaries were licensed along the Philadelphia Turnpike, an average of very nearly one ordinary per mile. One license was issued to a business concern, Benjamin Burk & Son, and fourteen licenses were issued to individuals, two to women and twelve licenses to men.

The old tavern, situated on the turnpike at the head of Bird River near Mile Post 12, was called the Twelve Mile House in 1850 and the Jacob Gerst Tavern in 1877, the structure now at 10848 Philadelphia Road. In 1813, Benjamin Henry Latrobe stopped at the Red Lion Inn, situated at the head of the Bird River thirteen and a half miles from Baltimore, the inn originally built in 1760 and known at different times as the Stone Tavern and Skerrett's Tavern.[76] Either Thomas Christopher or Charles Carnan may have operated the old inn in 1831.

---

[76] Inventory of Historic Properties, BA-257. Maryland Historical Trust, Annapolis, Maryland.

Back River Neck Road

Mile Post	Licensee	Year	Approximate Location
8	Richard Paine	1830, 1831	Mace Avenue
8½	Elisha Coe	1830	Rossville
10	Daniel Anthony	1832	Barrison Point Road
11	Ann Freburger	1831	Cedar Point Drive

The original Back River Neck Road began at the Philadelphia Turnpike near Mile Post 5½ and went in an easterly direction to the village of Rossville, near the intersection of Mace Avenue, Stemmers Run Road, and Rossville Boulevard, the old village largely north of the railroad tracks. The original alignment mostly now is gone, but a portion of the old road remains today as Golden Ring Road. From Rossville, the original Back River Neck Road turned in a more southeasterly direction generally along present-day Stemmers Run Boulevard and Back River Neck Road to Barrison Point Road about Mile Post 10. The old road was not operated as a turnpike.

Richard Paine was licensed both as an ordinary and a trader at Mile Post 8 in the old village of Rossville. In 1831, Elisha Coe, probably the same man licensed at Mile Post 8½ near the Philadelphia Turnpike in 1830, was licensed as an ordinary at Mile Post 8½, at or near Rossville. Daniel Anthony was licensed as a trader at Mile Post 10, near the end of the old road, near the intersection of Barrison Point Road. One woman, Ann Freburger, was licensed as an ordinary at Mile Post 11, at or near the very end of the road. With four licensed ordinaries, the old road averaged roughly one ordinary every three quarters of a mile.

Middle River Neck Road

Mile Post	Licensee	Year	Approximate Location
9	Nicholas Grimes	1831	Orem Road
14	William Jones	1830, 1831	Carroll Island
18	George Waller	1831	Rossville (?)

The original Middle River Neck Road began at Rossville near Mile Post 8 and headed generally in an easterly direction, approximately along the present-day alignments of Orem Road to about Mile Post 9½, Eastern Boulevard to about Mile Post 11, and Carroll Island Road to about Mile Post 14. The old road was not operated as a turnpike.

An ordinary license was issued to Nicholas Grimes at Mile Post 9, about one mile east of the village of Rossville, near the intersection of Orem Road and Old Orem Road today. A second ordinary license was issued to William Jones at Mile Post 14, near the end of the road at Carroll Island. A third ordinary license was issued to George Waller at Mile Post 18, about three miles out in the Chesapeake Bay, the clerk apparently erring in recording the mile post or even the name of the road. If his correct Mile Post was 8 instead of 18, George Waller was located at Rossville. With three licensed ordinaries, Middle River Neck Road averaged just one ordinary every two miles. No traders were licensed on the old road.

Other Locations

Canton

Now situated well within the city limits, Canton in 1831 was adjacent to the city, south of Highlandtown, and had its own post office. Ordinary licenses were issued to Robert Woodward, one mile near Canton; to Thomas Littlejohn, three miles near Canton; and, to William A. Thompson, at ½ Canton White House, the descriptions too cryptic to determine the locations of the three ordinaries more precisely than at or near Canton. Surprisingly, no traders were licensed in Canton or in nearby Highlandtown.

Franklinville

Franklinville was a small village on the west bank of the Little Gunpowder River, approximately midway between present-day Philadelphia Road and Bel Air Road. Franklinville Road began at Bradshaw Road near Mile Post 14½ and headed in a northeasterly direction toward the village at Mile Post 16. One trader license was issued to Upton Reid at Mile Post 16. No ordinary licenses were issued at Franklinville.

Trappe Road Turnpike

Today, Trappe Road extends only from Merritt Boulevard to North Point Road. However, in 1831, Trappe Road began at the Philadelphia Turnpike in Orangeville near the Pulaski Highway and Kresson Street intersection, about Mile Post 2½; headed in a southeasterly direction generally along the alignment of Dundalk Avenue to its intersection with O'Donnell Street and German Hill Road, near Mile Post 4; turned south onto Holabird Avenue, about Mile Post 4½; headed east generally along Holabird Avenue to Merritt Boulevard, at about Mile Post 6; then generally followed its present alignment, ending at North Point Road at about Mile Post 6½. An ordinary license was issued to Mary Mayzo at Mile Post 5, near the intersection of Delvale and Holabird Avenues today. A portion of the road was operated as a turnpike, with a toll gate on what was then Fifth Avenue, but now is Holabird Avenue about Mile Post 4.

Franklin Turnpike

The old Franklin Turnpike began at the Frederick Turnpike, just east of the Gwynns Falls, near Mile Post 2½, following the present-day Franklintown Road, nearly paralleling the east bank of the Gwynns Falls, heading north and west, crossing the river just west of Hilton Street near Mile Post 4, following the Dead Run tributary to the village of Franklin (called Franklintown today), at about Mile Post 5½, just inside the present city limits. Along the old turnpike, Paul Rust was licensed as an ordinary and a trader at Mile Post 4½, near Wynan's Way today. The woolen works owned by the firm Charles & John Wethered was licensed as a trader at Franklin.

Central Race Course

Built by the Maryland Jockey Club in 1831, the Central Race Course was located on the first old Frederick Road, now Johnnycake Road, near Ingleside Avenue, the most prominent and popular of all the race tracks around Baltimore, holding races featuring the most noted thoroughbreds of the day.[77] Ordinary licenses were issued to Charles Goddard, John Shipman, James M. Selden, Lewis Robinson, Theron Barnum, and Martin Weble, near the old race rack, all six licenses issued in October on a prorated basis, strongly implying that the race track opened about the same time.

---

[77] Scharf, J. Thomas, *History of Baltimore City and County.* Louis H. Everts, Publishers, Philadelphia, Pennsylvania, 1881.

Susquehanna Railroad

The Baltimore and Susquehanna Railroad Company was chartered by an act of the state legislature dated February 13, 1828, authorizing the construction of a railroad from Baltimore to the Susquehanna River. The following year construction commenced, by 1831 reaching Cockeysville. Through several acquisitions and mergers, the company long operated under the name of the Northern Central Railroad. Ordinary licenses were issued to James Walsh and Cornelius McCann, both at Mile Post 1½, about four or five hundred yards north of North Avenue along the Jones Falls, apparently not along the Falls Turnpike, but close. An ordinary license was issued to John R. Gwynn at Mile Post 4 on the Baltimore & Susquehanna Road, presumably the Susquhanna Railroad, possibly near Cold Spring Lane.

Daniel Wiegant was licensed as an ordinary at Mile Post 1½ on the Rail Road, but which railroad unrecorded. If he was located on the Baltimore and Ohio Railroad, then he probably was situated near James Walsh and Cornelius McCann

An ordinary license was issued to Henry G. Brown at Mile Post 31 on the railroad, probably near the old Oakland Station, just south of the Pennsylvania border at the intersection of New Freedom Road and Oakland Road today.

Ellicott's Mills

In 1830 and 1831, a trader license was issued to the firm Jonathon Ellicott & Sons at Ellicott's Mills. With the dissolution of the firm Ellicott & Company in 1812, the property was partitioned, Jonathan Ellicott receiving the Patapsco flour mills, located close to where the

Frederick Turnpike crosses the river, operating the Patapsco Mills by Jonathan Ellicott & Sons.[78]

Union Manufacturing Company

The Union Manufacturing Company was established in 1808 with capital of $1,000,000, the state one of the shareholders.[79] The company owned extensive land just upstream of the Patapsco Mills on both sides of the river. In 1832, a trader license was issued to the company at Mile Post 10.

Warren Factory

The Warren factory was a cotton mill located on the Gunpowder River, east of Cockeysville, near where present-day Warren Road crosses the Loch Raven Reservoir. An ordinary license was issued to Joshua Cross and John Harryman at Mile Post 14, William Duncan at Mile Post 14½, and Jonathan M. Wilson at Mile Post 15, all four near the Warren Factory. In 1831, a trader license was issued to the Warren Company at Mile Post 14 at the Warren Factory, long since inundated by the reservoir.

Oakland Factory

The Oakland Factory was a cotton mill and a thriving little village located on the North Branch Patapsco River about one mile north of

---

[78] Evans, Charles V., *Biographical and Historical Accounts of the Fox, Ellicott, and Evans Families, and the Different Families Connected with Them.* Press of Baker, Jones & Co., Buffalo, New York, 1882.

[79] Scharf, John Thomas, *History of Baltimore City and County, from the earliest period to the Present Day.* Louis H. Everts, Philadelphia, Pennsylvania, 1881.

the Liberty Turnpike, now submerged by the reservoir.[80] The firm Samuel Morton & Son was licensed as a trader in 1830 and again in 1831 at Mile Post 18 at the Oakland Factory.

Miscellaneous

In 1830, Mary Pickett was licensed as an ordinary at Mile Post 4½ on Hillen's Road, close to the intersection of Hillen Road and Woodbourne Avenue today.

Elizabeth Barthower was licensed at Mile Post 1½ on New Cut. That mile post places the lady's ordinary just north of the old city boundary, then along North Avenue, between Payson Street and Baltimore Cemetery, but no street or other land mark named New Cut has been found on any early maps. In 1830, a woman named Elizabeth Berthaur was enumerated as the head of household in Baltimore's First Ward, whether the two women were one and the same uncertain, no one by either surname in the city directories in 1829 or 1833.[81]

Today, Dover Road begins near Upperco on the Hanover Turnpike near Mile Post 22 and goes in a southeastern direction, ending at Butler Road, about two miles west of Falls Road, at about Mile Post 18. An ordinary license was issued to Robert Alder at Mile Post 18 on Dover Road, at or near the small village of Dover. Today, Dover Road picks up again at Tufton Avenue about Mile Post 15 and continues south until it ends at Green Spring Avenue. Formerly, Dover Road was continuous from Upperco, through Dover,

---

[80] Scott, Diana Mills, *The Forgotten Corner, A History of Oakland Mill*. Historical Society of Carroll County, Westminster, Maryland, 2005. Inventory of Historic Properties, CR-30. Maryland Historical Trust, Annapolis, Maryland.

[81] 1830 Census, First Ward, Baltimore City, Maryland, Page 30. National Archives and Records Administration, Washington, DC.

continuing south until it crossed the Falls Turnpike about Mile Post 9. A trader license was issued to Caleb Bishop at Mile Post 13, at or near the intersection with Ridge Road.

The Valley Paper Mill was located on the Little Falls of the Gunpowder on Valley Mill Road, just north of Rayville, about twenty miles from Baltimore. A trader license was issued to John Devries at Valley Mills.

Mine Run Mills was located on First Mine Branch at Hunters Mill Road just northeast of Hereford. In 1830, a trader license was issued to Peter G. Hunter there, the present-day road apparently named after the owner and not the mill. The following year, he again was issued a trader license near Wiseburg, about two miles from Mine Run Mills. A trader license was issued to Benjamin Lesourd near Hunters Mill.

The Powhattan Factory, a cotton manufacturer, was located on the Gwynns Falls, in a small village called Powhattan, long since gone and now on the property of the Woodlawn Cemetery. A trader license was issued to Richard Pearce at Powhattan.

In 1830, a trader license was issued to Amos Earp at Mile Post 8 on Old Forge Road and to Amos Harp at the same location in 1831, probably the same man. The trader possibly was located near St. Joseph's Catholic Church on Bel Air Road in the vicinity of Old Forge Lane.

A trader license was issued to James S. Wilson at Long Green near Copper Factory. Long Green remains a small village located where Manor Road crosses Long Green Road today. Copper works formerly were located near where the Harford Turnpike crossed the Gunpowder Falls, about three and a half miles to the southeast as the crow flies.

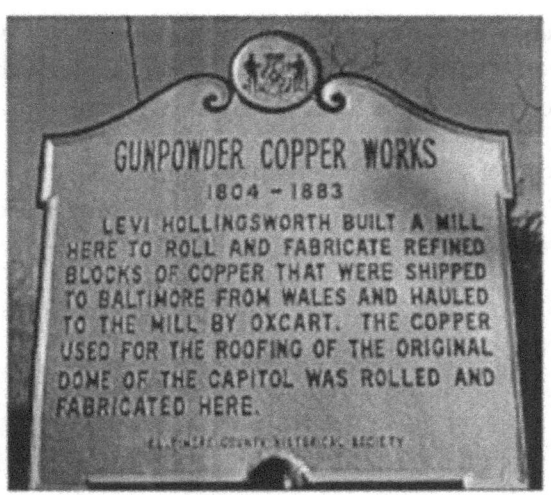

In 1831, Thomas Galloway licensed his ordinary at Mile Post 11 on Furnace Road. Today, no road by that name or any similar name has been found in Baltimore County.

In 1831, trader Richard Owings was licensed at Mile Post 9 on Court Road, now Old Court Road, about one mile south of Reisterstown Road, near the Beltway overpass.

In 1832, Samuel Sparhawk was licensed at Mile Post 18 near Sumwalt's Mill, the modern location long since lost to history.

In 1831, trader Samuel J. Gainson was licensed at Mile Post 14 on Manor Road, at or near the small village of Long Green. Charles Murden also was licensed on Manor Road at Mile Post 18, near the Jarrettsville Pike.

Trader Elisha Carman was licensed at Mile Post 14 on Joppa Road, but Joppa Road runs roughly west to east about ten miles from the courthouse, his location along Joppa Road uncertain.

Trader John Davis was licensed at Mile Post 18 on old Landing Road. Today, Old Landing Road is a mere fragment of the old road near

Joppa leading to a landing on the Gunpowder River; however, because the mile post places John Davis in Harford County, the old road probably connected Joppa Road to a nearby landing.

A trader license was issued to William Mallahein at Mile Post 19 at Patapsco Falls, probably the tributary of the North Branch Patapsco River, just upstream from Finksburg, very close to the Carroll County border.

Index

Adams, 23, 44
Alder, 22, 103
Algire, 16, 60
Allen, 5, 9, 10, 12, 46, 47, 49, 94
Allison, 13, 18, 75
Ambrose, 14, 71
America, 12, 86
Anthony, 11, 97
Arnold, 12, 18, 34, 94
Bacon, 15, 75
Badders, 19, 76, 80
Bailey, 5, 6, 45
Baker, 7, 11, 16, 60, 61, 64, 66, 87
Barnett, 9, 14, 19, 46, 48
Barnum, 21, 100
Barthower, 15, 18, 103
Batson, 18, 67, 69
Battee, 5, 7, 12, 15, 91, 92
Beckley, 6, 11, 78, 80
Bell, 85
Belt, 64
Berthaur, 103
Bigham, 22, 46
Bishop, 10, 13, 18, 20, 86, 87, 91, 104
Blackwell, 5, 6, 52
Blatchley, 12, 15, 75
Bond, 7, 17, 26, 78
Bonham, 19, 44
Bowen, 17, 72, 73
Bowers, 14, 18, 19, 26, 56, 75, 91
Bramwell, 8, 60
Brandt, 12, 94
Brinkman, 63
Brochans, 7, 96
Brockam, 16, 94, 96
Brookens, 12, 96
Brookhard, 17
Brookhart, 14, 77
Brooks, 9, 11, 26, 82
Brown, 11, 20, 44, 101
Bryan, 15, 16, 78, 84
Buck, 10, 14, 19, 25, 87
Buckingham, 7, 10, 49, 70
Burk, 5, 8, 13, 17, 60, 63, 94, 96
Burnham, 5, 7, 12, 16, 72, 73
Burton, 5, 9, 12, 87
Cable, 18, 67
Campbell, 22, 34
Canoles, 17, 87
Carman, 9, 105
Carnan, 22, 94, 96
Carr, 22, 39
Carter, 13, 15, 47
Caton, 73
Chambers, 8, 47
Chapman, 5, 6, 7, 54, 63
Choate, 6, 25, 50, 53
Christopher, 7, 94, 96
Clarke, 10, 20, 76, 82, 85
Cockey, 6, 10, 25, 67, 68,

72, 83
Coe, 12, 15, 95, 97
Coleman, 8, 68
Conn, 17, 21, 53, 58, 77
Conoway, 20, 46, 48
Cook, 14, 18, 46, 47
Cooper, 1, 7, 79, 80
Corbin, 19, 67
Cornelius, 8, 17, 76, 82
Cox, 11, 64, 78
Craig, 14, 79
Crist, 19, 60, 65
Cromwell, 15, 33
Cross, 22, 102
Crouse, 18, 76
Crumrine, 22, 61
Cullimore, 22, 86
Curley, 22, 34
Davis, 10, 19, 25, 61, 64, 105
Day, 6, 89, 91, 92
De Groff, 17, 39
Decker, 56
Dendy, 18, 75, 82
Devries, 5, 6, 8, 36, 104
Dillon, 20, 40
Downey, 11, 36
Driver, 6, 15, 39, 45
Ducker, 6, 8, 54, 55
Dugas, 9, 46, 49
Duncan, 21, 102
Durham, 11, 22, 71, 73
Dwyer, 10, 53, 57
Earbaugh, 22, 68
Earp, 9, 104

Ebaugh, 8, 61, 64, 65
Eichelberger, 18, 76
Elder, 22, 36, 37
Ellicott, 5, 8, 39, 40, 41, 101
Ertman, 16, 86
Everhart, 7, 23, 61
Ewing, 8, 18, 26, 78, 80
Farmer, 13, 34
Fedemyer, 10, 39, 44
Feelemyer, 13, 38, 44
Ferney, 12, 17, 54, 56
Fisher, 14, 18, 54, 56
Foon, 12
Ford, 7, 13, 15, 26, 38, 43, 45
Forester, 22, 36
Fowble, 64
Fox, 10, 44
Frank, 64
Franklin, 15, 91
Freburger, 14, 97
Freed, 19, 62
Freeland, 17, 76
Frelemyer, 19
Frick, 22, 61
Fridge, 43
Frost, 14, 17, 52
Frush, 56
Fuller, 12, 91
Gainson, 8, 105
Galloway, 11, 22, 26, 105
Gamble, 14, 18, 39
Gardner, 18, 61
Garey, 5, 6, 20, 47, 70
Garner, 5, 7, 8, 53, 67, 68

Garrett, 13, 18, 78
Geiman, 57
Gelbach, 6, 14, 26, 86
Gerst, 96
Gibbs, 13, 19, 71
Gill, 8, 72
Gilmor, 89
Gist, 18, 61
Goddard, 21, 100
Gore, 56
Gorsuch, 5, 7, 10, 52, 77, 83
Grace, 88
Gray, 6, 9, 12, 14, 17, 18, 39, 40, 87
Great, 21, 53, 57
Green, 6, 10, 14, 19, 26, 47, 77, 80
Griffin, 13, 19, 52, 55, 59
Grimes, 16, 98
Grove, 18, 53
Gwynn, 11, 18, 21, 71, 74, 101
Hague, 12, 86
Hall, 10, 71, 92
Hamilton, 18, 75, 82
Hamlin, 22, 43
Hanesworth, 20, 34
Hannagan, 20, 34
Hardy, 23, 38
Harker, 11, 22, 25, 87
Harlan, 6, 15, 38, 43
Harp, 5, 104
Harrison, 9, 15, 39, 50, 61
Harryman, 9, 11, 53, 102
Hartley, 20, 47

Hartzell, 13, 18, 53, 57, 67
Hawkins, 14, 19, 94
Heibly, 63
Henshaw, 13, 87
Heston, 11, 63
Hively, 22, 26, 60
Hoffman, 10, 14, 16, 38, 80, 82
Hollins, 9, 71
Hoover, 6, 72
Horner, 18, 67, 69
Houck, 7, 17, 61, 62, 66
House, 14, 17, 38
Hugo, 22, 91
Hunt, 17, 73, 77, 84
Hunter, 6, 9, 16, 79, 84, 104
Ilgenfritz, 12, 52, 58
Indik, 20, 52, 58
Jameson, 5, 7, 10, 17, 46, 67, 68
Jarvis, 6, 38
Johns, 5, 8, 72
Jones, 10, 12, 16, 21, 78, 86, 98
Kaase, 15, 94
Kauffman, 7, 78
Kelly, 10, 15, 21, 70
Kennedy, 14, 75
Keplinger, 16, 94
Kidd, 20, 86
Kilbourne, 9, 77
King, 7, 12, 15, 22, 26, 52, 53, 58, 77, 80, 91
Kuntz, 14, 26, 67, 68
Lafferty, 20, 44

Lamott, 18, 22, 61, 64, 72
Larpenter, 13, 16, 52
Latrobe, 96
Leaf, 5, 17, 72, 73
Leamon, 13, 38, 43
Leef, 1, 10
Lehman, 19
Lemley, 16, 86
Lesourd, 7, 104
Lewin, 20, 52
Lewis, 17, 86
Lilly, 20, 46
Linsley, 12, 17, 91
Little, 12, 15, 47, 48
Littlejohn, 14, 99
Litzinger, 11, 21, 71, 73
Lowe, 85
Macklan, 10, 20, 71, 73
Mallahein, 10, 106
Mallonee, 16, 72
Manning, 5, 8, 20, 26, 53, 67, 68
Marsh, 16, 77
Marshall, 20, 22, 79, 80
Martin, 12, 75, 87
Maxwell, 13, 17, 75
Maydwell, 19, 71
Mayzo, 12, 15, 100
McAllister, 13, 16, 52, 58
McBlair, 6, 9, 91, 92
McCann, 23, 101
McCauley, 12, 15, 94
McCleary, 15, 38
McClure, 16, 87
McCoy, 21, 72

McElhert, 8, 53
McGurk, 20, 44
McHanney, 20, 60
McIlvaine, 21, 61
McMechen, 13, 39
McSherry, 13, 19, 52
Medairy, 56
Merford, 11, 76
Merryman, 9, 72, 82
Michael, 7, 79, 80
Miller, 13, 16, 21, 26, 61
Milner, 15, 52
Minnickhyson, 10, 95
Mitchell, 15, 86
Moale, 64
Moon, 15, 71
Mooney, 13, 91
Moran, 1, 13, 17, 20, 26, 75, 86
Morris, 9, 39, 43
Morrison, 20, 71
Morrow, 8, 17, 53
Morton, 6, 8, 9, 14, 26, 78, 80, 103
Motter, 5, 7, 61
Mumma, 18, 76
Mungan, 12, 19, 71
Murden, 10, 25, 105
Murphy, 20, 53
Murray, 17
Murry, 8, 60, 94
Musselman, 22, 60
Neukirk, 15, 91
Null, 17, 60
Odell, 6, 49

Onion, 13, 19, 95
Oram, 22, 36
Orrick, 11, 82
Oursler, 63
Owens, 6, 15, 38, 43
Owings, 5, 7, 13, 15, 39, 43, 46, 48, 50, 105
Paine, 5, 7, 12, 16, 97
Parlett, 7, 16, 17, 87, 90
Pearce, 7, 104
Peden, 8, 71, 73
Penny, 9, 46, 48, 50
Perigo, 13, 76, 82
Pernie, 21, 87
Perrigo, 5, 7, 16, 26
Phelps, 10, 44
Phipps, 22, 75
Pickett, 14, 21, 103
Pierpoint, 11, 39
Plowman, 21, 82
Porter, 9, 20, 70
Price, 5, 7, 9, 77, 82
Quigly, 68
Reid, 5, 7, 99
Rhoades, 14
Rhodes, 11, 19, 39, 43
Richards, 65
Riggen, 12, 75
Riggin, 16, 86
Ringrose, 10, 20, 44
Roads, 13, 17, 33
Roatbaust, 20, 61
Roberts, 12, 21, 38
Robertson, 21, 38, 43, 67
Robinson, 13, 17, 21, 43, 100
Roe, 5, 7, 78
Rogers, 16, 26
Rust, 6, 15, 100
Rutledge, 18, 78
Scott, 7, 11, 72
Selden, 21, 100
Sewell, 12, 86
Shealey, 17, 76
Shipley, 5, 47
Shiply, 7
Shipman, 21, 100
Shoemaker, 19, 34
Showers, 16, 62
Simpers, 11, 72
Slade, 14, 15, 77
Small, 19, 79
Smith, 14, 19, 34, 39
Smyser, 14, 16, 17, 78, 84
Smyzer, 76
Sparhawk, 11, 105
Sparks, 5, 13, 79, 90
Spindler, 8, 78
Standiford, 9, 18, 78, 82, 85
Stansbury, 6, 8, 10, 55, 64, 68
Stapleton, 6, 12, 15, 94
Starr, 12, 15, 75
Steele, 48
Sterns, 13, 39
Stick, 13, 16, 60, 63
Stone, 13, 38
Storm, 22, 53
Strickert, 12, 91
Stubbins, 14, 17, 77

Taney, 23, 67
Tayman, 14, 22, 26, 52, 55, 58
Thomas, 8, 53
Thompson, 5, 14, 21, 39, 61, 99
Tipton, 5, 8, 12, 16, 19, 72, 77
Tongue, 14, 15, 39
Tracey, 8, 75
Tress, 13, 15, 46
Trump, 50
Turner, 9, 79
Ulrich, 16, 79
Uppercou, 7, 60
Vanhorn, 8, 13, 94
Voltz, 20, 26, 46
Wadlow, 9, 47
Waggoner, 8, 52, 58
Walker, 13, 19, 76, 83, 85
Wallace, 5, 13, 76, 82
Waller, 22, 98
Walsh, 16, 101
Walter, 12, 21, 38, 45, 87
Walters, 11, 46
Ward, 6, 8, 11, 14, 19, 46, 47, 50, 67, 68
Ware, 6, 8, 9, 17, 47, 49, 76, 82, 85
Washington, 79
Watkins, 7, 13, 16, 87, 88, 90
Weaver, 12, 17, 18, 54, 62
Webb, 5, 7, 12, 16, 77, 80, 82
Weble, 21, 100
Welch, 5, 6, 52, 59, 70
Wentz, 12, 16, 62, 63
Westerman, 9, 77
Wethered, 9, 100
Wheat, 8, 34, 35
Wheeler, 22, 87
Wiegant, 17, 101
Wier, 10, 21, 82, 85
Willingham, 12, 15, 86
Wilson, 7, 8, 17, 22, 75, 78, 84, 102, 104
Wise, 84
Wonn, 10, 46
Wooden, 8, 60
Woods, 21, 60
Woodward, 13, 17, 99
Woolry, 21, 68
Worley, 12, 18, 76
Wright, 5, 6, 45
Yeager, 17, 71
Young, 5, 6, 18, 21, 26, 47, 67
Zeney, 1, 14, 76
Ziagler, 22, 38, 43
Zimmerman, 5, 7, 80, 82
Zouck, 16, 72

www.ingramcontent.com/pod-product-compliance
Lightning Source LLC
Chambersburg PA
CBHW070931160426
43193CB00011B/1650